Yes Sisters

Yes Sisters

Surrounding Yourself with
Women Who AFFIRM, ENCOURAGE,
and CHALLENGE You

ANGELIA L. WHITE

with Erin Keeley Marshall

Revell

a division of Baker Publishing Group
Grand Rapids, Michigan

© 2020 by Angelia White

Published by Revell
a division of Baker Publishing Group
PO Box 6287, Grand Rapids, MI 49516-6287
www.revellbooks.com

Printed in the United States of America

Library of Congress Cataloging-in-Publication Data
Names: White, Angelia L., 1970– author.
Title: Yes sisters : surrounding yourself with women who affirm, encourage, and
    challenge you / Angelia L. White with Erin Keeley Marshall.
Description: Grand Rapids : Revell, a division of Baker Publishing Group, 2020.
Identifiers: LCCN 2019028440 | ISBN 9780800735883 (paperback)
Subjects: LCSH: Christian women—Religious life.
Classification: LCC BV4527 .W466 2020 | DDC 248.8/43—dc23
LC record available at https://lccn.loc.gov/2019028440

Published in association with Books & Such Literary Managment, 52 Mission Circle, Suite 122, PMB 170, Santa Rosa, CA 95409-5370, www.booksandsuch.com.

20 21 22 23 24 25 26   7 6 5 4 3

For the amazing loves of my life, who are my constant joy and who motivate me to be the best example of hope I can be as I aim to inspire women to believe in themselves and to know God loves them for who they are.

Contents

Acknowledgments

My goal in life is to speak hope to other women in order to empower and inspire them. My mother is the one who did this for me. She has shown me more love than I ever thought possible and taught me what it means to believe in yourself and pursue your passions. Because of her, I don't let others get me down, I fight for the things I believe in, I *fight for myself*, and I continue to let hope and love guide me in all that I do. She is a woman who spreads love to everyone she meets, and one of my biggest goals in life is to do the same.

I'm also incredibly grateful for all the amazing women who have believed in me through every season of my journey and who have spoken truth and *yes* into my life. Because of these strong and courageous women, I was able to keep pressing forward when I wanted to give up. They picked me up when I stumbled and fell, and I wouldn't be where I am today without their unfailing love and support.

What Is a Yes Sister?

She isn't always the one saying, "You *should* do this" or "You *should* do that" or correcting your grammar, but she will tell you if you have broccoli in your teeth. She's a woman in your circle who believes in you, who offers encouragement, insights, love, and wonder.

She is

- honest,
- encouraging,
- a confidante,
- trustworthy,
- loving,
- fun,
- nurturing,
- positive, and
- uplifting.

She is not

- catty,
- haughty,
- two-faced,
- lazy,
- selfish, or
- passive-aggressive.

She does not

- insist on being right,
- gossip about anyone,
- abuse flattery,
- nitpick mistakes, or
- strive to be seen as superior to you.

Yes, she does

- partner in prayer,
- offer fashion advice,
- appreciate you,
- gently nudge you, and
- celebrate you.

She makes you feel alive and sometimes has more confidence in you than you have in yourself. Her words and presence stir your soul toward greatness.

PART 1

Yes
to Believe

Chapter 1

We CAN Be Ready

For all of God's promises have been fulfilled in Christ with a resounding "Yes!" And through Christ, our "Amen" (which means "Yes") ascends to God for his glory.

2 Corinthians 1:20 NLT

My first glimpse of the azure sea took my breath away. I pressed against the passenger-side window of the car, trying to capture the vast expanse of water from the quick glimpses between buildings and palm trees as my friend Cheryl and I drove toward the waterfront.

"There it is," Cheryl said from behind the wheel. She is one of my closest Yes Sisters, and on this day, she understood what this trip and seeing that water meant to me.

After more than forty years on this earth, I had never seen the ocean. I'd imagined this moment countless times, and I'd nearly convinced myself that seeing the ocean on film or in a photograph was good enough. It wasn't.

Cheryl drove to the hotel she'd booked for us and pulled into the parking garage. We were in Tampa, Florida, for a weekend business retreat that Cheryl had organized with a few other women from our mastermind group. I didn't feel as polished or as intelligent as the other women. I barely scraped together the money to fly from Indiana after Cheryl invited me by saying, "You get yourself down here, and we'll take care of the rest." Regardless of how I felt compared to the other women, I knew God had brought me these women and this moment, and I wasn't about to miss it.

After parking the car, we headed straight for the beach so Cheryl could be with me for this big moment.

Tears of joy escaped the corners of my eyes as we walked toward that grand view of blue beyond the white sand. The waves curled and rolled toward the beach, and the water stretched to the horizon, where a vast sky reached upward and over our heads. The beauty astounded me.

"Let's take off our shoes," Cheryl said as we stepped onto sand so bright I needed my sunglasses.

"I can't believe it. It's amazing." I marveled at what I saw and found words inadequate to describe it.

I took off my shoes and sank my feet deep into the soft, warm sand until only the coral polish on my toes peered through the grains of white. The air was balmy on this November day and filled with the scents of salt and flowers. People in swimsuits were stretched out on towels and beach chairs. Children laughed and screamed as they jumped in the waves and dug into the sand. This certainly was not like a November day in Indiana.

Cheryl and I reached the water's edge. The rhythmic rolls of waves uncurled onto the sand with a frothy foam running up the beach. The cool water hit my feet and wrapped around my ankles. I wanted to cry and laugh with joy, and I did a little of both. This moment was so profound to me because of the journey it had taken to get here. I felt amazed when I thought of all God had done to bring me to this day. The satisfied smile on Cheryl's face affirmed what I felt inside. I thought, *Look how far you've come, girl!*

This day was about much more than seeing the ocean for the first time. It felt like it bridged moments and small decisions from decades past. So many experiences in my life easily could have blocked this day from ever happening. Moments filled with pain, disappointment, and sorrow. I hadn't taken perfect steps, and I'd made plenty of mistakes I was still learning from. I knew that I also had hard choices still to make—life-changing choices with enormous consequences. But without taking the small, tough steps in the past, I wouldn't have been standing on that beach in that moment.

I recalled a time a few years earlier when I'd spoken words that were certainly part of getting me to this ocean day. I was talking to a man whose tone and words expressed his disgust with me.

Chris wanted to shake me up, hurt me, and make me view the world as he saw it. For months, he'd been taking advantage of me professionally. I'd shared with him my dream for a magazine that offered hope to women. I was just getting the magazine off the ground, and I frequently mentioned how I wanted to build it and how much I still needed to learn. He took advantage of my naïveté and convinced me to pay him to help me out. In only a few months, I lost thousands of dollars that hadn't helped progress the magazine or brought in revenue. I learned a painful but valuable lesson with Chris. During a phone call, I told him I couldn't afford his expensive help any longer. I just didn't have the money, but I was going to figure out how to accomplish this dream anyway.

His response was hate-filled. He spewed, "If the only thing you have is hope and faith, but no money, then you don't have anything." Suddenly, I understood this man was tangled up in his own unhappiness.

After an encounter with challenging people, my best words usually come later and too late. But during that phone call with Chris, I spoke from my heart. The words were like a roar from within that brought me to the moment years later when I could celebrate with my good friend on the beach, sinking my toes into the soft sand as the warm waves washed over the tops of my feet.

"You're wrong," I said to Chris. "If I have hope and faith, that's *all* I need. I have everything!"

These words probably sounded like pure foolishness to him. But to me they were a spoken declaration of faith and I swelled with excitement as I said them. I didn't realize it then, but I was speaking my own loud "yes" to myself, to God's plan for my life, to a day when I'd see the ocean for the first time, and to so much more.

I never imagined the role a few women, my Yes Sisters, would play in boosting my faith, healing my spirit, and growing my courage to pursue my heart's greatest desires.

Friendship

My trip to the beach was a milestone in its own right. But sharing the event with my Yes Sister Cheryl quadrupled my joy. If it weren't for her strength and her pushing me when I needed it, I might still be waiting to see the ocean.

I had no idea the immeasurable gifts Yes Sisters would contribute to transforming my life and helping me realize my dreams.

Why do I call them Yes Sisters? Is there a difference between a friend and a Yes Sister?

The word *friend* conjures different images, from little girls in dress-up clothes to adventurous old ladies on a greeting card to women laughing together or leaned in close sharing secrets over coffee. Imagery of friendship is filled with joy, laughter, meaning, hugs, adventures, comfort, and always love. Friends make life richer. We need friends, and we need to be a friend.

As a little girl, I yearned for close friendships. I imagined what it would be like to have a sister or a sister-friend. I grew up with two older brothers but longed for companionship with a girlfriend who would help me decide right from wrong, boost my spirits when I was down, laugh with me, and let me confide my heart's deepest desires. I watched other little girls, imagining what it would be like to be their friend. Dolls, jump rope, hopscotch, slumber parties, college roommates, maids of honor . . . friends for life.

One day when I was six years old, I told my mom, "Someday I want a whole bunch of friends!"

The response I'd hoped to hear wasn't the one I received. I wanted my mother to say that, of course, I'd have more friends than I could count. My mother has been a Yes Sister to me throughout my life. But on that day, she spoke what felt like a great big "no" to me.

"Oh, Angelia, you're only going to have one or maybe two close girlfriends in your life. Hope for that."

My heart sank at her words. Though she said them kindly, they felt like a cold splash of water in my face.

Only one or two close friends? Did all women have so few friends? Why was it so hard to find good friends in a world filled with people? I continued to long for close sister-like friendships throughout my childhood.

My mother was speaking from her experience. Mom had a few women friends from church and one lifelong friend she cherished. Too soon, she would lose her sister and sister-in-law, who had been her best friends. These relationships were all she'd wanted.

Mom also knew well the other side of female relationships. At six, I had not yet encountered the rivalries between women, the mean girls, the two-facedness, the jealousies, the betrayals, and all the other negative interactions between women that destroy what could be great. I didn't know friendship could be hard work or that some people can suck the marrow from your bones.

I later learned what my mom couldn't tell me. I met many girls and women who were anything but friends.

But I was also blessed with key Yes Sisters who helped change a lifetime of nos into the life I'd always wanted.

In addition to being a friend, a Yes Sister is a woman in your circle who believes in you, who offers encouragement, insights, love, and wonder. Her words and being stir your soul toward greatness.

As friends do, Yes Sisters know where we've been and who we are now and love us anyway.

They also act as lighthouse keepers who keep lit the torch that guides us toward the future God has for us. They relight the lamp when the waves of circumstance or past issues roll higher around us. When our own sight grows dim, they carry the vision of who God is creating us to be.

In addition to being wonderful friends with whom we love to spend time and swap stories about children, work, and love, these women help us become our best selves. In my life, God has used Yes Sisters to heal me when I've needed it.

By investing in me as a whole person—my faith, dreams, losses, victories—these women have loved me as I am while pushing me not to settle. They've shown by their thoughtful, honest questions that they notice me.

It's easy to feel invisible when circumstances bring us down and loneliness lingers. With beautiful persistence, Yes Sisters don't leave us to drift in isolation. When our faith is tested, they speak truth from God's Word.

They are trustworthy and always there for us. Always.

These many years later, I have exactly what I'd hoped for: a whole bunch of friends! And more Yes Sisters than I could have dreamed possible.

We need different women for different seasons of life. And we serve a beneficial role for our friends through the waves of their seasons too. A good friend expands our world, introduces us to new experiences, and grows our compassion factor. One friend can never meet all our needs. We can't meet all of a friend's needs either.

Whenever I hear a woman say, "I've got two friends and I'm cool," I want to implore her to gather more friends close, to open her arms and heart to a wide circle of friends, diverse in every way. We need one another.

It's important to surround ourselves with friends—and Yes Sisters—who will make sure we always remember how valuable and how valued we are, and that *no* won't be the only word we'll hear.

Freedom from No

For most of my life, I woke up, did what others expected of me, went to bed, and repeated the sequence the next day. I loved my family and did my best to obey what I heard from the church pulpit. I have always valued kindness, both as the giver and the recipient.

But I was functioning on empty. The fact is, too often my needs for love and security and kindness remained unfilled. I went through the motions of living. My spirit, however, had dried up from unkind, unsafe input from others, even people I trusted to love me.

Childhood trauma had crippled my expectations for myself, and those early wounds were reflected throughout my adult life as I continued to accrue fresh battle scars.

I call those wounds—old and new—*nos*. They embody all the negative feedback that drags us down and makes us not take our hopes seriously, much less prioritize or pursue them.

I did daily life. That was about it. Even typing those words now, my fingers twitch for more.

I was stuck. Sure, I wanted more. I grieved my marriage and wished my husband and I could share our deepest desires and cheer each other on. I yearned for a safe church community with believers who acted in love instead of slinging hurtful rumors. I longed to feel beautiful and cherished. And I wanted to make a difference for someone else.

But I did not know my heart could heal and be filled. And I certainly did not understand how much God wanted those blessings for me.

I had never really thought in terms of nos. I had always sensed something was holding me back, but I didn't know what, and I certainly couldn't put a name to it.

Before I could discover the power of yes, I had to understand and name the nos that had trapped me. Key women in my life helped me do just that. Their support still points me toward freedom.

It took hearing the truth from strong women, Yes Sisters who paid attention to my heart, to identify how and where I'd let negative experiences and feedback steer my life. My sisters cracked open the door to the world of freedom that God had designed for me.

Nos can come in many forms, from any direction. The hurts I'd been dealt as a child were especially powerful and had gotten in the way of my dreams well into adulthood. They had shaped so many of my thoughts about myself that I was unable to recognize unhealthy relationships as an adult.

Nos do that. They get in the way of what we've been created for. My Yes Sisters spoke truth to me that opened my eyes to the freedom I'd been missing for so long. Moving into a future of yeses required dealing with the nos, and the first step was to embrace the freeing power of forgiving the people who had hurt me.

Freedom of Forgiveness

At one time, I easily could have fallen into the trap of bitterness. I had been victimized in the past. As a little girl, I was abused by several adults, and the abuse continued for years. I lived mired in those memories and focused on how much the abuse and my abusers had stolen from me.

I was surrounded by closed and angry minds. Even the church I attended professed more crippling gloom and doom than real truth of joy and grace.

It's surprisingly easy to be angry, to live with self-pity, to wrap up in a cloak of negativity and cynicism. We find strange comfort and security in these things. But we are not free.

My responses to hurtful people changed as God began to heal my heart through the influence and inspiration of women He brought into my life. Their wisdom and how they modeled healed living provided a vision of what my life could be—how I could be whole, as God intended. Their guidance provided footholds that helped me move steadily forward instead of continuing to stagnate without hope.

After a while, I began to recognize the changes in myself. When someone caused me pain, I no longer let it burrow. With God's help, I forgave them and moved on from the situation and forward with my life. Forgiveness meant I was no longer a victim. I was a survivor, and I was free.

Our lives will always be a giant no until we forgive. This means forgiving even those who haven't asked us to. Because our offer of forgiveness is not about them. It's about saying yes to ourselves.

The Yeses Ahead

Much of what I've learned has been through trial and error—and from getting back up once more with scraped knees. I've met many people who are their own worst enemies. Some blame the world or God or a political party or someone, *anyone*, else for their problems. They view everything through a negative lens. They don't experience true joy or the wonder of God because they stand in their own way.

Before receiving the gift found in Yes Sisters—women who express an affirming *yes!* when we most need it—it's important we take an honest look in the mirror, open our hearts, cultivate an inviting spirit, have the courage to be vulnerable, and welcome the unexpected that sisterhood invariably brings. We don't transform in just one day or without effort, but it all starts with us.

We also need to risk saying yes to ourselves. That might sound frightening, paralyzing, impossible, awe-inspiring, hope-filled, or a mix of all the above. Let me offer you this encouragement: you are reading this book, which means you are already daring to trust that yeses are possible for you. Keep believing that truth, sister!

Each of us must be our own Yes Sister before true, deep sister-friendships are possible. Dealing with our own messiness releases us from its power. We're all works in progress who are still capable of making decisions that leave us works without progress.

First, we must have the desire and willingness to change. My tipping point came in the months following the death of my father and grandmother. Those losses opened my eyes to the brevity of life and became like a coiled spring that catapulted me from the sluggishness I'd believed was unchangeable. Their deaths clarified how much I longed to fully, finally *live*.

When I truly wanted change and wanted it enough to look honestly at my problems, a desire to do the hard work transformation always requires grew within me. I experienced transformation as I learned to nurture the positive and expel the negative, including self-pity and self-criticism. A negative outlook will never attract deep relationships or a joyful spirit. I learned to choose a positive attitude despite my circumstances.

I spent several hours at the beach with Cheryl that November day. We strolled along the water's edge, picking up seashells. We walked to the end of the dock, took pictures, and laughed and talked as the sun fell behind us. I wanted to capture every moment and hold them forever. But even while I knew that was impossible, a promising peace rose within me. I knew that although the day marked my first visit to the ocean, it would not be my last. More days like that one waited on my horizon. This was the first of a new chapter. God had so much ahead.

And it wouldn't have happened if I hadn't found a Yes Sister and allowed her into my life.

Over the years, Yes Sisters—whose yeses fed my courage and starved my fears—have encouraged me in every facet of life. They have helped me accomplish my dreams, renewed my thinking, and set me on a path of growth and transformation I'm still walking. But first I had to step away from the atmosphere in which I'd been living, where the only thing I heard was no.

A WORD FROM
a Yes Sister

Cheryl Pullins, *speaker, brand specialist, personal coach, and CEO of Cheryl Pullins International*

A Loss to a Yes

On a gorgeous October day in Central Florida, I was taking a stroll through a shoe store when I realized my phone kept buzzing. When I pulled it out, I saw that I had texts, social media messages, and voicemails.

"What in the world is going on?" With my heart beating fast, I punched in a phone number. As the caller's awful words landed on my ears, my heart plummeted. I raced toward the door so I could get outside before I lost it.

The news didn't seem possible. Two days after her fiftieth birthday, my best friend of seventeen years had died in her sleep.

I ran to my car and frantically called my husband at work, something I rarely did. In the middle of my hysteria, I struggled to say that Janice had died.

I first met Janice when I was swirling down to the lowest point of my life. Our children were in the same class together and we met at a school function. Our friendship grew as my marriage was in turmoil. She became my confidante. I told her everything that was going on in my life.

With no judgment, Janice allowed me to travel an emotional roller coaster through heartache and bad decisions. At every turn, good or bad, Janice was there. We often treated each other to dinners because it was our way of escaping the challenges in our lives. We could make each other laugh until tears streamed down our faces. We shared our dreams and aspirations even when neither one of us could see how they were going to come to life.

Janice was my Yes Sister. When my life started turning for the better, she was the first person I wanted to bring along. I wanted her to experience the freedom I was beginning to enjoy. The freedom to be me. To be who God wanted me to be in the world. I now felt a responsibility to be Janice's Yes Sister, even when she was saying no to herself.

On her fiftieth birthday, two days before she passed away, Janice and I exchanged text messages. We agreed that with her new decade, I would support her in living the life she truly desired. I was so excited. But that plan didn't come to fruition for Janice.

Janice's death changed me. It nearly broke me, but it also inspired me to keep going and be my best self in the time that I have. Because of her, I committed to saying yes to sisters who were on their journey and needed another sister to tell them they could do and be all they desire.

That's what being a Yes Sister means—agreeing with another sister that the life they truly want can be theirs. Yes, sister, you can do it. Yes, sister, you can become whoever you long to become. Yes, sister, you can inspire others to say yes too.

Janice's death encouraged me to live more fully for myself—and for others.

Chapter 2

We CAN Realize
Our Dreams

Now all glory to God, who is able, through his mighty power at work
within us, to accomplish infinitely more than we might ask or think.

Ephesians 3:20 NLT

Stretched out on the bathroom floor, I gripped my abdomen and
cried out for relief. *What is wrong?* I wondered.

"Mom, I can't pee!"

Somewhere in the fog of pain, I thought of my dolls lying hap-
hazardly where I'd left them in my bedroom minutes earlier. As a
young child, I just wanted to feel better so I could go back to playing.
Nothing bad ever happened in the world I imagined with them.

My mom thought I had a bladder infection, so she made an appointment for me to see a doctor. When we walked into the 1970s-
era office, the receptionist directed us to sit in the outdated waiting
room until we were called back to the exam room. After my exam,
my dad arrived and joined Mom and the doctor in a separate room.
I could see them through a glass window but couldn't hear what

they were saying. What was Dad doing there? Why were they talking about me but wouldn't let me hear? Was I really sick?

I didn't understand what the fuss was about. So I sat and waited, staring through the glass, with no idea why my mom looked so confused. Soon the doctor and my parents came back into the exam room. The doctor's first question was whether anyone had touched me inappropriately.

"No." My heart quickened as the word spilled out.

Could this pain really have something to do with The Secret? I'd never breathed a word about it because I would get in trouble. I was a good girl who didn't snitch.

But the doctor and my parents kept asking questions—personal, embarrassing questions. I squirmed at the attention. Especially about this.

The doctor looked concerned. Mom looked worried. And Dad stood there, watching me with an expression I didn't understand. What would he think of me?

I shook my head. "No." My answer was more subdued that time.

Deep inside, my heart pounded harder and my stomach churned. *No!*

* * *

So much life passed between that long-ago day as a little girl and the day I felt true freedom breathing ocean air for the first time. Much like your story, mine has included plenty of ups—like the births of my three children and *HOPE for Women* magazine. Four dreams come true.

But also like you, I have weathered my share of downs as well, an excess of nos in my life. Hits to my self-worth over many years stunted my understanding of my true identity, my purpose, and my capabilities.

The dreams of our hearts—the ones instilled by God—do not die. But they can be starved and buried alive. My big dream, the one that tapped my shoulder from time to time, longed for life for many years. I grew weary assuming I had to shush it. But it never stopped whispering to me.

And then one day a Yes Sister spoke the yes I craved. Her encouragement breathed life into me and lifted me out of the graveyard of no.

Defining Moment

I was sitting in church in my hometown of Muncie, Indiana, when I felt God speak to me. It was 2005. Both my grandmother and my father had passed away earlier that year.

I found myself grieving their deaths, but especially in the case of my dad, I mourned that he'd wasted so much of his life. I'd often wondered if it was his upbringing or the effects of Vietnam that had turned him toward substance abuse. His dream had been to retire and collect Social Security. That was what he constantly talked about. It had become his message. That June he would have received it.

Now he was gone, and there was no chance to redeem his talents and hopes. No time to build a greater legacy than the wish to collect Social Security. My father's life was a mirror to my own. I wasn't living with vitality. Was I wasting my life too?

"Look around you, Angelia," the Lord seemed to say. "These people are not really living. They're just existing."

That marked the moment I started my journey to pursue my larger purpose.

I felt an urgency inside me. I wanted my life to mean something, and I wanted to reach the end of life content with what I'd done. I didn't *want* simply to fulfill an ambition; I *needed* to act on the calling of my heart.

The first tangible part of that pursuit was to create a magazine. Several years earlier, I'd met with an industry professional about the idea, and he had encouraged me to go for it. I'd been excited after the meeting. But then I didn't pursue the idea any further.

Now was the time.

I didn't have a degree or any experience.

I didn't know how to start.

I had only a passion.

Many people told me that starting a magazine was impossible. What did I know about publishing? What experience did I have? Who was I to think I could do it?

But a deep inner desire had been stirring in my heart for years. I loved the idea of encouraging other women and having a place where we'd be encouraged together. Many options for such a place existed, but my heart was always about a magazine.

Decades of personal hurts paralyzed me with doubts. The negative voices came, but when I told my sister-in-law Terri about what I wanted to do, she told me to move forward. "I know you can do this," she said.

That was all I needed. Her yes pushed me to keep going.

Tentative First Steps

First, I dove in and created a newsletter. I put together an email list of nearly a hundred women I knew and thought would enjoy it. The newsletter included all sorts of encouraging thoughts and stories. I felt certain other women were experiencing the same challenges and questions I was. I wanted to be an encouragement to all women longing for God, even if they didn't know that's what they were hungering for. If we could connect and share our stories, even more women would be encouraged.

About this time, a friend gave me *The Dream Giver* by Bruce Wilkinson. I also devoured Rick Warren's *The Purpose-Driven Life*. I started reading, believing, and working, and things started happening. I made connections with other women online, and my newsletter grew in just a few months.

My friend Tracy wrote me and said, "By the response you're getting, you know you're supposed to do the magazine."

Another nudge from the Lord.

I met with the same magazine publisher who'd encouraged me years earlier and told him everything that had happened since we'd last spoken. He seemed to catch my determination and was generous in sharing his thoughts and ideas.

"I want you to dig deep, really deep, and find out what message you should be sharing based on your own experiences." His words held more wisdom than I understood at the time.

I nodded and felt an ache in the pit of my stomach. Self-examination and looking deeply into the truth of our lives is painful and not always pretty. But discovering the wonder of how God creates beauty from each no requires us to first unearth them. He doesn't waste any hurt and desires to heal every one of them, for our good and to prepare us to build up others.

I did what the publisher said and dug deep in a way I didn't want to. I thought about the years of sexual abuse. The pain in my marriage. The disappointments. The hurt. How my devotion to God hadn't always been as strong as I wished.

What did these have in common?

As I thought about all this, I felt God drop a message into my spirit. *Hope.* I needed hope. I knew other women needed it too—all women, actually. We all need hope for everything we face. This was the theme of my magazine even before I had a magazine. It was the theme and purpose of my life.

After that meeting, everything moved quickly as I connected with other women and learned about publishing. Before the year was done, I had launched *HOPE for Women.*

Dreaming with Wild Abandon

As children, we dream with wild abandon. The world shines full of wonder in even the simple things. Then we grow up.

The years between our innocent childhoods and disillusioned adulthoods are filled with the wear and tear of growing up—disappointment, teasing, bullies, heartbreak, humiliation, cynicism, and the cruel realities of evil let loose to harm and destroy us. While there's no ceiling to a child's imagination, outside sources begin to erode that wonder.

Joy is mocked. Ideas, clothing, or behavior that are out-of-the-box spark snickers and disdain. We begin to hear the word *no* about our dreams and visions.

No is a necessary word when we're young. Our parents tell us no to protect us from harm or unwanted situations. And then once we learn it well, we laughingly run around as toddlers saying no to every direction from our parents.

As we get older, the weight of the word feels much heavier—*no*, that boy won't go to the dance with you; *no*, you can't stay out past curfew; *no*, you can't attend that college; *no*, you aren't hired for this job. The number of times I've heard no seems infinite.

Without realizing it, we can begin to own the word as our birthright. We might even use it as a wall of protection against more pain and disappointment.

But *no* does not determine our worth. God wants to show you and me how to give Him the nos and watch Him transform our lives with all the yeses He created us for.

When Dreams Turn to Reality

Our words are powerful. I know people always say that "actions speak louder than words," but we shouldn't overlook the influence our words can have. Words can certainly bring us down, yet they are also able to inspire and encourage us, especially when the words affirm that those around us genuinely believe in us.

Negative voices have stopped generations of women from rising above their circumstances to follow the God-given spark in their hearts. Society, culture, religious dogmas, gender expectations and restrictions, and controlling relationships have all contributed to keeping millions of women from pursuing their purposes and growing into their best selves. But the truth is that any woman can remain gracious, lovely, kind, warm, and loving while also being strong and driven. Power is at its best when it builds beliefs, provides opportunity, and strengthens others.

It took me many years to learn that truth. Before that day in church in 2005, I allowed the nos to affect me. I had started to believe life was a series of nos strung together—a new one waiting for me around every corner. I couldn't foresee opportunities for me to grow and thrive and become the woman I was meant to be. Essentially, hopelessness consumed me.

It took the Lord and incredible women to show me how big one little word can be: *yes*. Along the way, Yes Sisters kept me going when I wanted to give up.

They reminded me that *yes*, I am strong; *yes*, I can overcome obstacles; *yes*, I can survive the storms of life; *yes*, I can make a difference; *yes*, I am loved; *yes*, God can use me to do *big* things; and, *yes*, they will always be there for me, pushing me to believe in myself.

In 2006, all that pushing paid off, and my dream to create a magazine became a reality when the first issue of *HOPE for Women* was printed. As I held that first copy in my hands with Cece Winans on the cover, I felt like crying. My dream was now a reality.

Starting a magazine from scratch and running my own business had been no simple task. It took a tremendous amount of dedication. I was sometimes in tears and completely overwhelmed. There were late nights (there still are!) and hours upon hours of what seemed like endless work. It was daunting. I questioned more than once if I was going to be able to keep up that pace, asking myself if all the blood, sweat, and tears were worth it.

Then I was overcome with the reminder that not only had my dream become a reality, but who I was had changed through the process. I still had many things to learn and many tough times ahead, but I knew without a doubt that I was on the right path. Over the years, that knowledge has only grown. And one of the greatest surprises has been how much I've been given through the process. My hope has been strengthened through bringing hope to other women.

It's true that real life has a way of crushing our secret dreams and our childhood visions.

But it doesn't have to be that way.

You can live your dream!

Are You Ready?

Are you ready to pursue *your* fullest life? Or are you already in the trenches and in need of some encouragement? Gather the sisters! Some of the best Yes Sisters for encouraging a dream are those who are currently working and living their own. When I finally verbalized the secret desire of my heart—to launch a magazine that offers women hope—my sister-in-law was one of the first people to tell me I could do it. As more sisters encouraged me along the way, their voices spurred my passion to keep going. I realized successful people have had help along the way, and they'll often help others in turn.

How do you know whether you should follow an idea or a dream? The following things might be an indication that you should:

- You feel joy when you think or talk about it.
- When you hear about other people doing something similar, you have an inner longing and excitement about it.

- You've had the dream (even a secret one) for a long time and it's never faded.
- You might have had a sense of it as a child, before "growing up" took it away.

As you pray consistently, seek God with all your heart and ask Him to reveal what you should do. Listen to His quiet voice. What is He saying to you? If you still don't know, gather your Yes Sisters and start praying together for the answer.

These things should not stop you from pursuing your dream:

- Someone tells you it's impossible or a pipe dream.
- It is very hard and seems beyond your current abilities.
- You've failed at it in the past. Remember, failure is part of the process.
- You are not qualified or don't have the education or experience you think you need.
- You don't have the money.
- You don't know how to proceed.
- You're afraid.

These are roadblocks in your journey. They are normal and part of pursuing something great. Trust that God will open the way. It's okay to feel like you're in the dark. Courage means doing something while being afraid. It doesn't mean you won't still feel fear; it means you'll keep moving forward anyway.

The first step in going after your heart's desire is saying *yes* to it!

Let me be one of your Yes Sisters through this book. I'm cheering you on. Gather other women who will believe in you and say, "You can do this!"

Because you can.

A WORD FROM
a Yes Sister

Cindy Monroe, *founder and CEO of Thirty-One Gifts*

Dreaming with Others in Mind

When Cindy Monroe founded Thirty-One Gifts, she was twenty-nine years old and had a husband and two young children. She also had a dream—to provide women an opportunity to earn extra income by running their own business and to empower and support them on their journey.

"I didn't set out to be an entrepreneur," says Cindy. "But in college, I took an entrepreneurship class that sparked something in me that stayed with me. I was always curious and creative, and years later, it all came together when I had a calling and an 'aha' moment, realizing there was a way I could help other women.

"I wanted to help women like me who were working or maybe home with children but wanted to earn extra money and stop living paycheck to paycheck. I wanted to find a way to help women help their families and improve their lives by having a way to earn enough money to enjoy family vacations, pay for essentials, or be able to donate and give back.

"I knew there were women like me who wanted to chase after their dreams and pursue their families' interests while also doing what they felt God wanted of them, like donating toward the building fund at church or going on a mission trip."

Cindy's dream came to life with the help of many others who were there for her along the way.

"God helped with the vision and the planning of it and has placed different people—many of them women—in the business for me to rely on. Women in our church family, as well as executive assistants I've had, our independent sales consultants, and others helped me define and grow the company. My sister was there for me with prayers, and she helped me come up with the name, based on the woman described in Proverbs 31. That woman not only takes great care of her family, but she also has her own businesses."

Founded in 2003, today Thirty-One Gifts is one of the largest direct-selling organizations in the world, offering purses and wallets, totes, home organization solutions and décor, thermal bags, jewelry, and more. The company, however, is about much more than its products. Thirty-One is a family of individuals who share a passion for empowering women and are committed to celebrating, encouraging, and rewarding others for who they are. The company has consistently held true to that original mission and today helps tens of thousands of women find success and satisfaction by running their own Thirty-One businesses.

Cindy's original mission remains her number one goal. By staying focused on it, welcoming help from others, and following God's plan for her, she's grown that dream into a reality that has helped thousands of women and families reach their dreams as well.

Chapter 3

God DOES Love Us

According to the riches of his glory [may he] grant you to be strengthened with power through his Spirit in your inner being, so that Christ may dwell in your hearts through faith—that you, being rooted and grounded in love, may have strength to comprehend with all the saints what is the breadth and length and height and depth, and to know the love of Christ that surpasses knowledge, that you may be filled with all the fullness of God.

Ephesians 3:16–19 ESV

The first step any of us take toward a dream is saying yes to it. But what if saying yes doesn't come easily? For many of us, it doesn't.

Even if our status quo isn't all we want, we often find mixed comfort in it because it's familiar. Saying yes to greater potential can feel daunting because it necessitates change. Change shifts us into unfamiliar territory, and the unfamiliar can be intimidating.

Saying yes leads to questions such as How do I get to my yes? and Why am I worthy of yes, and of beauty, value, and purpose?

You may think, *I want to say yes and live beyond the nos more than anything.* But how *exactly do I overcome them?*

I get it. Our long-held beliefs about our limitations can be tough as mountains to overcome. But going back to the very beginning always reminds me of the pathway through the challenges.

When He created you and me, God decided our value. He alone has the authority to do that. Psalm 139:13–14 says, "You shaped me first inside, then out; you formed me in my mother's womb. I thank you, High God—you're breathtaking! Body and soul, I am marvelously made!" (Message).

Building our lives on His love and learning to look to Him for our value guides us in knowing who we really are.

He is our Daddy, who loves us and heals us and gives us worth. He is the source of all yeses.

● ● ●

I never breathed a word of the childhood abuse I had endured until that day in the doctor's office. I'd been forced to promise not to tell anyone. But in one afternoon all that changed. What I'd kept raw and private inside was suddenly raw and known by others.

Sitting before my parents and the doctor, my soul exposed, I trembled with vulnerability. What would they think? Would they love me? I knew my mother would, but would my father look at me the same? Would he love me less? The adults kept their voices calm and kind, but they continued to ask questions, more and more questions that seemed to go on forever. Finally, they took me to the hospital for tests.

"Angie, what happened to you was really bad," Mom said. "We have to find the person who did this to you so we can make sure they don't hurt anyone else."

I looked at her. "Mom, am I gonna get a whoopin'?" That's all I'd thought the whole time The Secret had been buried inside me.

Her eyes widened. "No, of course not. We just need to know who did it."

Something about the kindness in her voice made me think I could tell her the truth and it would be okay. I told her about the man who had hurt me.

I'll never forget the look on her face. It was like she'd been led to the light and it all started to make sense.

Sexual abuse had been part of my story for a long time, since I was four years old, when several other adults molested me. It's common knowledge now that predators can spot victims who've already been abused. I don't know what singled me out, but I'd been living a nightmare I couldn't wake up from, holding in a secret that hurt as much as the abuse ever did.

This man always wanted to "help" my mom by babysitting me. He hung around the house a lot. One day he took my two brothers and me to the fair. Anytime we'd go anywhere with him, my parents would give him plenty of money to cover our expenses. When he took us to a jazz festival in Cincinnati, Dad gave him nearly a hundred dollars, which thrilled us kids because we knew we'd get to play lots of games, ride the rides, and buy candy.

But he took the money and played the games himself. We didn't go on a single ride or eat any candy. Nothing. After he spent all my dad's money and took us home, he put my two brothers to bed and then came into my room and had his way with me. As he often did.

After he was done, he would go back to the living room to watch TV and make himself comfortable in our house. He'd pick me up occasionally and present himself as a caring, loving person. But when we would go to the country to a place we called "the farm," he would molest me and others. No one suspected anything evil about him.

I was the first person in our family to say something. When I was older, I learned that these abuses had been family secrets for more years than I knew. After they were exposed, we finally began to talk openly about this part of our history.

After I left the hospital that day, I opened up more to my mother and finally shared all I'd been through. I told her about places the man would take me and more specifics of what I'd endured.

I could tell the abuse was even worse than she'd suspected. When we were finished talking, she stormed into the bedroom she and Dad shared. I knew she was going to tell him.

My mouth went dry and my palms grew damp. Minutes passed. I opened my door a crack to see if Dad would be mad at me.

The next thing I knew, their bedroom door crashed open and Dad burst into the hallway with his shotgun and shells. Mom tried to stop him, but because she was as small as she was, she couldn't do it. Dad looked ready and determined to go kill my abuser, all because of me.

● ● ●

The enemy loves to pound us with false guilt. At that impressionable age, I didn't know if I might be partly to blame for the abuse I endured. Shame weighed heavily on me, making me feel not so much *un*lovable as maybe *not quite as* lovable. The experience was emotionally damaging all the same.

I thank the Lord my dad didn't let his anger get the better of him, or I might have lost him along with my innocence. Because Dad loved me, he responded instantly to defend me. I'd been so scared and unsure whether I'd still be okay in his eyes. But his actions made it obvious that I was still his little girl, and all he wanted to do was fix things—or at least get justice for me. I felt the power of his love.

My imperfect human father's response to my brokenness provided a glimpse of how much more God, my heavenly Father, loves me.

For some of us, it's easy to imagine Jesus as gentle and caring. Almighty Father God, however, might seem aloof, angry, and vengeful. But He is the one who sent Jesus to us. God the Father loves us as we are, and it was not okay with Him to leave us broken and needy. It still isn't.

His love isn't merely a vague kindness toward humanity. He doesn't yawn and tolerate us. He dearly loves us—and not just *us*, but He loves *you* and He loves *me*. It's very personal for Him, and for us.

Your story is personal to Him.

There's no hiding from Him. He knows all the nos and all the fears that fool us into believing we aren't worthy of a beautiful life of yeses.

Possibly a lot like yours, the path of my life steered me far from understanding God's love for a long time. What I imagined doing, who I imagined being, was kept beyond my reach. I didn't have much reason to take it seriously.

And old shame lingered like a pest. If we aren't rock-solid sure that we are loved, wounds and all, we avoid being fully known by others. We hesitate to let our guard down for fear of more trouncing to our spirit. Shame doesn't let go without a fight, and it loves to kick us when we're down. It circles back around to ridicule our identity and God's heart toward us.

I've had to unpack a lot of hurt and shame to enjoy the freedom to pursue my dream. The process has taken time, and it's still ongoing. We never stop growing.

Actually, that's a great thing, because our worn-out places are God's opportunities to undo the negative messages we've received and recreate our lives beyond what we imagined. That's the healing power of His love.

Always with Us

My Yes Sisters have shown me complete love in the midst of chaos, confusion, questions, and unfinished business. Young and old, of all ethnicities, from a wide range of economic and educational backgrounds, nearby and long-distance, they have lifted me with their words and been a safe refuge for my heart.

They've also challenged and encouraged me not to remain resigned to less than God's best for me. They've pointed me toward what needs tending—things that have been crippling and holding me back. And ultimately, they've pointed me to God's love for me.

Looking back, I can see that He has pursued me all my life. When I was eight or ten years old, I first started to understand that I need Jesus. One of the first Scripture verses I ever memorized was Revelation 3:20, which says, "Behold, I stand at the door and knock; if any one hears my voice and opens the door, I will come in to him and eat with him, and he with me" (RSV).

I gave my heart to Jesus, and even then, I knew something had transpired in my life. I believe it was the touch of God.

I think I've always known logically that He loves me. However, it took a long time for me to learn that He delights to pursue me. What a difference that distinction makes.

He doesn't love us out of obligation; He *loves* to love us.

What about Pain?

Many of us wonder how God can love us if, in our worst situations, He doesn't immediately get us out of them. Why did it take decades for me to break free from what was destroying me? Why didn't He rescue me sooner?

Even though our lives are about choices and occasionally we make unwise ones, many people suffer completely apart from anything they did. Abuse is not the victim's fault. Not ever. I don't believe for a second that the Lord wants us to remain in an abusive situation.

We wish He would eliminate everything bad from our lives. But we live in this world and we're faced with its obstacles. Demons. Forces that want to destroy us and take away our confidence in God.

God is the Healer of every pain and heartache. But the loving process of His healing can hurt as He cleans out our inner wounds that have festered.

He even allows the pain caused by our own sin to help us understand the depth of His love for us. Throughout Scripture, God didn't shield people from every pain. His goal has always been redemption, daily and eternally, for all of us. He didn't shield himself from sin and death but took every bit of it on Himself to save us.

Eventually, the miracle of His love transcends all our wounds.

Trust in His love frees us to adopt His view of us. We feel empowered because we are His. He can use the ashes of our bad experiences to mold and shape us, creating beauty from every bit of what remains—for His purposes, for whatever time and season.

How can I be so sure? I watched Him do it in my life.

A WORD FROM
a Yes Sister

Cara Whitney, radio personality and author

No Bones about It

To say that someone has skeletons in their closet means they have done something they don't want other people to know about. We hide these skeletons because we fear that our past actions will change other people's perceptions of us.

Maybe that's why I used to feel like I needed to "clean up my life" before considering that God could love me just as I am. Many people assume Christianity is only about attending church, performing rituals, and not committing certain sins. That is not Christianity.

True Christianity is a personal relationship with Jesus Christ. God knows what is in each one of our closets. He even knows our thoughts.

But instead of feeling insecure about that truth, it gives me hope because, despite my dirty life, He still wants a relationship with me. Even better is the fact that He says if I turn from known sin, He will wipe my slate clean.

Jesus's death on the cross must have seemed to the disciples like a total failure. But there is no greater success story than what happened three days later. The resurrection transformed the grief of the disciples into hope and joy.

Because there are *no* bones in Jesus's tomb, there is no need to worry about the bones in my closet. Christ's resurrection makes a success story possible in the lives of all who believe.

> For God so loved the world that he gave his one and only Son, that whoever believes in him shall not perish but have eternal life. For God did not send his Son into the world to condemn the world, but to save the world through him.
>
> John 3:16–17

Chapter 4

We ARE Beautiful

> You are altogether beautiful, my darling.
>
> Song of Solomon 4:7 NLT

The carpet was even more ruby red than it had always looked on television.

All around me, a sea of Versace, de la Renta, Dior, Armani, and other famous designer creations decorated the celebrities who mingled as if it was just another day in the life. I was starstruck—and then I saw Oprah!

And there I was, fresh off the plane from central Indiana. Was I really here?

This was my experience in 2018 at an awards gala in Dallas. It was an honor I'll never forget.

I looked down at my gown and smoothed a nonexistent wrinkle. This haute-couture world of perfect bodies, name-dropping, and big bank accounts was not one I frequented. I felt like royalty and wasn't sure what to do with that emotion.

Fake it till you feel it, they say. I breathed deeply and inwardly cheered myself on.

Even though I felt out of place at first among so many VIPs, my heart was humbled and at peace to realize that I fit just fine. I had worked hard and earned my place there.

Like my first weekend at the ocean, that awards night marked a milestone for me. I socialized with others who were living their own dreams, and no one questioned my right to be there. After a while neither did I.

My reason for getting dolled up was as valid as theirs, and my questions about whether I belonged lived only in my head. So I let go of my insecurity, shed my nerves, and freed my brightest smile to wear itself out all evening long. *I felt beautiful.*

That feeling wasn't about reaching a certain social or economic status. It had nothing to do with being seen with certain people or trying to fit into a size 0 gown, good gracious. I hadn't taken on a new fitness regime. Hadn't lived on lettuce and lemon water for a year. No plastic surgery.

I'd grown. The evening's beauty came from a deeper place in me that for too long had stagnated with unrealized hope.

When I looked in the mirror while I was getting ready before the event, I saw the real me. The miracle began from within, and it's been an exquisite healing.

Beyond Body-Beautiful

Aside from the array of products we use to make ourselves look our best on the outside, it's easy to find a wide array of supplements and fitness routines to detox our insides from the yuck we accumulate from the environment, food, and aging. All of that may be great, but something else within us might need a detox too—our spirit.

I used to muddle through the fog of my unhealed heart. But I've experienced more "detoxing" of my spirit than I knew was possible, or more accurately, *possible for me.*

The detoxification makes room for truth and hope about who Jesus says I am. I'm awakening to the truth of my identity as never before. Maybe I couldn't appreciate it while life kept me stuck.

Spiritual detoxing involves recognizing what has clouded our lives and getting the help we need to stop living as its victim. The process happens gradually as we call the nos what they are and reframe our thinking to align with what God says about us.

That's difficult to do on our own, and it's precisely where healthy Yes Sisters can help. My Yes Sisters have set me straight time after time about true worth and beauty. Yes Sisters speak words of growth. They lovingly get in our space with the truth, so to speak, because they care so much.

That's Sarah's story.

Sarah's lifestyle proclaims her commitment to health and beauty. Her discipline is beyond rival when it comes to exercising every day and refusing a second bite of dessert. Organic produce fills her refrigerator, and she invested in the top-rated whole-house water filtration system.

Her alarm clock rings at 4:30 seven mornings a week so she can fit in an hour-long workout before dressing in designer suits and tackling the rest of the day. And every January she schedules a year's worth of monthly spa appointments. No way graying roots will ever show on *her* head! Regular facials keep her skin silky smooth.

The problem, though, is Sarah also must schedule two chiropractor appointments each week to help her back recover from weight lifting too much at the gym. And she fits in weekly visits to her therapist to cope with stress and aging, as well as perceived past failures and the pressure to hang on to twentysomething looks at forty-three.

All of *that* is in addition to her prescriptions to treat an ulcer and chronic anxiety because of a high credit card balance, which she racked up from indulging in pricey gel mani-pedis, shopping only at expensive boutiques, and installing that amazing water-filtration system.

You might be smiling or cringing by now. But are you weary like I am from reading about her beauty regimen?

Sarah's relief from this unhealthy lifestyle came in the form of a Yes Sister she met in a graduate night class. Sarah admired Diane's gracious aura from a distance, and her respect grew when the women got to know each other better while paired for a research project.

Diane looked several years older than Sarah. She dressed attractively but simply. And although she wore little makeup, her eyes and smile lit up the room. One evening when Sarah mentioned her workout routine, Diane merely nodded.

"Raising three teenagers doesn't leave much time for exercise," Diane admitted. "But I do enjoy bike riding with my family. And we often have our best talks while walking around the neighborhood."

Diane added, "I don't mind my bit of belly pudge. I'd rather enjoy family time than hours on my old elliptical machine." She smiled as she talked about a recent camping trip with her husband, kids, and longtime friends from church.

"You're really very pretty," Sarah told her. "How do you keep your glow? I'm exhausted keeping up with just myself!"

Diane laughed. "Thank you. I think you are a beautiful woman. But I'd be tired too if . . ."

She seemed to consider whether to continue. After a moment, she did. "A long time ago, my grandmother sat me down and told me about the balance of beauty. She made me promise to always pay more attention to my insides than my outside. It sounded backward at the time. But I'm thankful she set me straight early on. If we aren't filled on the inside, efforts to keep the outside shiny wear thin."

The advice might have sounded offensive coming from most people. But Diane's gentle words touched something deep in Sarah, as if the woman saw straight into Sarah's unsettled heart. It brought her immediate relief she hadn't felt since she was a little girl. She didn't want to try so hard. All her hard work hadn't silenced the memories of taunts and fat jokes she'd heard from other kids growing up. She wanted Diane's style of beauty, which was so freeing to be around.

In that moment, Diane became one of Sarah's best Yes Sisters.

● ● ●

It's taken decades for me to get here, to this season I hope never ends, because I feel more alive and whole than ever before. I'm living proof that what is healed on the inside naturally enhances the beauty on the outside.

People tell me I have a new light about me, a visible peace and tranquility. They usually say this with a sense of awe. Not that they are surprised by this light, but they are transfixed, fascinated by the transforming power of true healing. That kind of healing is real and lasting beauty.

Let's be honest, most of us don't have extra time or funds or physical trainers to turn us into runway-ready models. And while we're being truly transparent, let's admit that most of us don't have the genes that lend themselves to a red-carpet career.

That's just fine, because any of us normal Janes can grow in inner loveliness. This richer beauty transforms our appearance with a radiance that shows brighter by the year. It's an attractiveness that leads those around us to wonder at the joy we exude.

My Yes Sisters are gorgeous women. Style fashionistas? Some of them. Physically stunning? To me, they are. But their hearts hold their real beauty.

Cheryl encouraged me to find a signature piece of jewelry. It didn't have to be expensive, just something that celebrated my style. She also guided me to some of her favorite stores and helped me find two classic items every woman needs: a little black dress and red lipstick.

My friend Nancy told me to always dress like I am going to work in an office, even when working at home.

"When you get up and get dressed, you're more productive," she said.

I'll always be grateful for their friendly tips to help me look my best. We women need to do that for each other.

But the thoughtfulness behind their practical encouragement is what means the most to me. When any one of my sisters shows me, or anyone else, kindness, they make the world lovelier.

Yes Sisters build into, raise up, encourage, and empower others without the drama of veiled one-upping. They love to lift each other to live above shallow image-consciousness.

Yes Sisters pursue and celebrate the potential in other women. They thoughtfully seek what's below the surface. They give honor to the special beauty in someone else.

Ruffled Bedspreads and Red Carpets

Along with honoring each other's unique beauty, we need the "special" in other areas of life.

When I was young, my mother saw to my needs as her only daughter, which included adding personal touches to my space. She flipped through the JCPenney catalog and found a yellow (my favorite color) satin bedspread set complete with a bed skirt and shams—and ruffles all over. Mom made sure there was beauty in my life that uniquely fit me.

Whatever your personal version of a ruffled yellow bedspread may be, special touches of beauty matter. They celebrate life and, in their own ways, point to the rare loveliness about us.

My growing-up world was not fancy, but beauty doesn't need to be fancy. When my mother gave me that bedspread, she did more than keep me warm while I slept. She saw my desire to feel special, and she validated the beauty inside my heart.

Several of my Yes Sisters have reinforced this idea. In my work, I benefit from all kinds of expert advice from them. They show me by example the strength in being comfortable in my personal style and valuing my own attractive qualities. They've helped me see the importance of bringing beauty into our surroundings. God created women specially to reflect His beauty in and around us.

When I moved into a new apartment, I made sure to fill it with special touches that meant something to me. By then I'd learned from close friends that the environment I dwell in matters, as does dressing for my role.

Yes Sisters help us reframe misguided patterns that life has programmed us to believe. As a grown woman who, for years, rarely felt celebrated for anything, I don't have adequate words of thanks for my sisters who have taken special notice of me.

They have taught me to cherish the special, to celebrate it. By living with that in mind, we embrace healing. We act as cheerleaders for one another as God heals our broken parts. And we bring beauty to life.

Beauty of Brokenness, Beauty of Healing

The beauty of the healed. It's amazing.

One of the most stunning aspects of healing is its source, its beginning. Healing begins in brokenness. There is no healing without brokenness. There's beauty in brokenness because of what it leads to—the potential for life change carried in its shards.

Brokenness shows us how needy we are. Discomfort jump-starts our cravings and longings, two powerful needs ripe for fulfilling.

Pain guides us somewhere, always. Some people follow it down a dark road, seeking comfort in lesser "fixes" like drugs, bad relationships, or other dependencies. Others follow it to a dead end, giving up and losing all hope.

And a few others let it do its authentic work of guiding them to our Creator, who has the authority to give us true identity. He alone knows exactly how to work beautiful healing over time, every time.

Instead of casting us off as hopeless cases, the Lord picks up every tattered piece of us and goes to work reforming us as His masterpieces. He delights in us and in the process.

Everything that is beautiful did not necessarily begin that way. It's said that a broken bone heals to become stronger than it was originally.

When Jesus heals us, we are stronger than before the nos shook us. Better able to hold more beauty and reflect the Lord's unfading hope. Better equipped to understand the brokenness of others. He fills us with the glow of His Spirit, a holy glow that everything else can only mimic.

And then wholeness leads to new depths of gratitude and a healthy ability to love ourselves, to practice the power of forgiveness, to discern when to say no, and to grow the desire to share that beauty with others. Yes Sisters have modeled all of these things for me.

It took me a long time to step out in faith. God had years of work to do in me, piles of garbage to free me from. My life is now marked by peace and happiness. I know who I am and what I want. I'm no longer afraid to embrace and live each moment. It's a miracle to watch Him work, to feel and see Him create more good than I could dream of on my own.

I no longer tolerate things that don't matter, and I want to embrace the beauty of living free of unnecessary drama. No energy spent on grudges. No private, inward nurturing of familiar old ways of living that only keep me down. God has a similar miracle of growth for you, whatever beautiful form He wants that to take in your life.

My colleague Eileen told me how her Yes Sister Rachel once pointed out a mindset that was keeping her from fully living.

They were eating lunch together one day in college, chatting about *this plan* and *that hope*, when Rachel set down her fork. Her eyes narrowed sternly, but her mouth curved in a good-natured smirk.

"You focus a lot on the future." Rachel did not speak harshly, but she wasn't offering a compliment either.

Do I really? Eileen hadn't ever considered that she might be missing out on present joy.

Her thoughts crystallized throughout the afternoon. It was true. She lived subconsciously, wishing for an idealistic future of greener grass than the current humdrum of tests, essays, labs, and homework.

Many years later, Eileen still checks her focus when discontent comes knocking. She's certain she will seek out here-and-now blessings more for the rest of her life, all because of a truth-telling Yes Sister.

Yes Sisters bring beautiful growth!

God created our bodies to heal, and He created our spirits and souls to heal as well. He knows how to recreate us, how to bring about art from each of our stories, even when the healing process itself stings.

If you feel delayed in your healing process or aren't yet aware of the beauty in your life, know these things are possible for you. We all have detoxing work to do. Everything doesn't shift and get fixed instantly.

Come clean with God. Be real about your reality, that secret that embarrasses you and makes you want to hide in shame. That's exactly where God wants you to experience Him.

God pinpoints those areas and works with precision. Trust that He is working in you all the time, even when the progress seems slow or nonexistent or you face repeated setbacks.

Some of the worst things end up guiding us to the best things.

Look for the beauty He's put inside you, no matter how small or insignificant it might seem at first: the warmth of your smile, the way you tell a story, the tug on your heart when you know someone is hurting. Those everyday qualities will grow to enormous proportions and make you unique and strong.

YES, *you are beautiful.*

A WORD FROM
a Yes Sister

*Angela Guzman, contributor for Thrive Global,
media enthusiast, and lover of words*

Beauty in Grief

For a long time, I struggled with the concept of beauty. I believed I had to have everything figured out, and oftentimes I envied the women around me. I would wallow in self-pity and wonder why my life wasn't beautiful. I didn't have parents who loved me. I didn't have a cinematic college experience. I didn't have the career I dreamed about.

Becoming a mom changed me. It was the reality check I desperately needed. Gazing at my child, I saw beauty within my life and myself. I have friends who have become my family. I have a husband who adores me. I have work moms who nurture and love me.

God has strategically placed these beautiful souls in my life, and I wouldn't be who I am today without them. I had and have so much that I took for granted.

Recently, my heart was broken again, and the idols associated with beauty weighed heavy. I had a miscarriage, and the connotation associated with the word *miscarriage* haunted me. The word sounds like I did something wrong—I *miss-carried*.

Instead of succumbing to this ugliness, I decided to navigate through the grief and find the hidden beauty. I've discovered grace and appreciate life in a way I never thought was possible. My beauty is imperfectly perfect.

I am so grateful for the women the Lord has placed in my life. They've all played a role in helping me find beauty within grief.

Chapter 5

We ARE Worthy

We all, with unveiled face, beholding the glory of the Lord, are being
transformed into the same image from one degree of glory to another.

2 Corinthians 3:18 ESV

Have you ever received a gift, large or small, so thoughtful that it
brought you to tears?

My favorites have been unexpected notes or a text from a friend
saying she's been thinking of me and asking if I'm doing okay. The
"check-ins" that let me know I'm worth considering touch my heart
most.

An employee of mine wrote to tell me I've been a blessing for
giving her a platform to share her writing. I'm still not sure she
understands what a blessing her words were to me! One unassuming compliment, and I walked around all day feeling worthwhile.

We need those types of gifts that can't be wrapped up with a
bow. Gifts that counteract the times someone's insensitive comment knocked us over with shame.

We need those gifts, because even as adults, it doesn't take much negative feedback to remind us of old hurts and reduce our feelings of worth.

Blasts from the Past

When I was a child, I retreated into quiet reserve and didn't speak up for myself. Isolation became a coping mechanism to deal with the abuse and shame. I'd play with my Barbies and make them have their own little family, the perfect family. I created a make-believe person I wanted to be because the person I saw myself as was marred by abuse.

In my imagination, I was a pretty, light-skinned girl with long, beautiful hair rather than a brown-skinned girl with medium-length hair. No abuse happened in my make-believe family. Nothing bad diminished their beauty or value.

In real life, I felt so lacking. I had no idea of all God was preparing me for. He still is the God of Isaiah 61:3, "[who cares] for the needs of all who mourn . . . [and gives] them bouquets of roses instead of ashes, messages of joy instead of news of doom, a praising heart instead of a languid spirit" (Message). But back then, how I ached.

Fast-forward from my early experiences to years later when my kids were young. We didn't have money to cover the necessities, much less extras. A woman who supposedly cared about us told me my children's clothes looked dingy.

Her words tapped in to my memories of the bullies I'd dealt with in gymnastics as a young girl. I was talented, and I loved flying through the air upside down doing flips and cartwheels. Maybe they were jealous. Who knows what drove their meanness?

Anyway, several of my garments went missing. A special leotard my mother had bought for me disappeared. They stole my underwear and then told me I was nasty for not having it. Then they capped all that off with comments about my hair not being as pretty as theirs. They knew exactly where to fire their verbal daggers. Bullies have a knack for that.

To have similar unkind things said about my own children when I was doing my best to provide for them hit a very vulnerable place in me.

A number of years ago, I had to ask someone if I could borrow a small amount of cash to pay a phone bill, only to have them chastise me. That was in 2008, when the economy took a steep downturn and many hardworking people like me struggled financially.

That was just one event that topped off two decades of being treated as unworthy in a controlling church environment. I endured lies spread about me for years. My dream of starting a magazine was ridiculed. I was so accustomed to feeling beaten down that I stayed in that unhealthy place until a Yes Sister spoke the bold truth that I was not where I needed to be.

For many years, I lived dragged down by the languishing spirit Isaiah 61 describes. I carried a heavy resignation that the parts of my life that weren't working were the best I'd get. I believed the lies that I must have somehow deserved my circumstances and the abuses against me.

Our greatest enemy, the devil, employs shame as one of his most powerful weapons. He fires it at us every chance he gets. Like other bullies, he knows our vulnerable places well.

Worth, the Truth

But then God connected me with one life-giving Yes Sister after another. "But then God" is such a hope-filled phrase, isn't it?

I didn't know I had been stuck in a stronghold of lies about myself. I didn't know I needed truth. It wasn't as if I set out to look for Yes Sisters who'd tell me the truth, and I certainly didn't know where to find them.

God initiated it all. We don't have to have the answers to take the first step of believing that He has more for us. He knows who and what fill our days, and He will meet us there with people who can help. Most times, He sent Sisters into my current circumstances—writers, fashion experts, editors, women I interviewed, and other businesswomen. He built on each step I took in faith.

Until I stopped listening to the lies and started listening to Yes Sisters who pointed me to the truth in God's Word, the pain I experienced as a young girl continued to shape my view of myself and what I believed I did or didn't deserve. I was truly unable to see that God really did want more for me.

But Yes Sisters helped me believe I would not always feel broken. I was worthy of love and beauty, of yeses, and of being treated with kindness and respect.

They also modeled for me grace in the unknown, meaning unless we've been in someone else's circumstances, we have no clue what they're dealing with.

Yes Sisters choose to gift us with grace. And they keep choosing that path. They know everyone carries hurts no one else knows about. Through their example, they teach that grace and love change lives.

Both positive and realistic, they think the best of us and know we are doing our best. They hold on to this hope especially during (and not in spite of) the tough times when not much seems to be working out for us. They hold on for us when we feel like giving up. And most importantly, they redirect our thoughts to God, who cherishes us and promises to provide for us.

Sometimes it takes a Yes Sister in our corner to wake us up to these truths. We may play that role in another woman's life and experience the blessing of giving back.

Awhile back I worked with a woman who always seemed unhappy. She felt in bondage, held captive by circumstances that kept her from living free. Because of what I'd been through, I was able to understand her low moods.

I got to be a Yes Sister and encourage her. As she put her trust in God over a stretch of four years, I witnessed a visible change in her. Anyone who sees her now knows she's free.

No one but the Lord can define our worth.

Nothing bad that happened to us can diminish our worth.

Yes Sisters tell me this key thing: "You are worth more than this." We set the standard for how we expect to be treated—not in a selfish or demanding way but with a healthy, grace-filled, confident strength. The respect we show ourselves carries over into our interactions with others. Many people only treat us with the level of respect we show to ourselves.

During the early days when I was building *HOPE*, I didn't charge much for ad placement. I felt grateful that people wanted to put their ads in my magazine. It took Cheryl to reset some of my basic thinking about myself, which was carrying over into how I was running the company.

"Girl, you've got to stop giving these ads away. You're going to start getting what you're worth."

I didn't know what I was worth.

She said, "Think about the time and energy you put into your work. There's a cost associated with that."

She helped me see that I wasn't being demanding or pushy by expecting fair payment for the product I offered. I needed to stop letting people walk all over me or take advantage of my giving nature.

"You devalue yourself when you worry about what people will think of you," my Yes Sister Sonya Reed told me when I was being too soft on an employee who wasn't doing her job. "If people don't do what you're paying them to do to your satisfaction, then don't pay them. If you take your car to the shop but the mechanic doesn't fix it, he doesn't get paid as if he did. Right?"

It sounded so simple when she said it, but it took her truth-talk to validate my worth and retrain my thinking. She was another shoulder to lean on as I learned to walk with my head high.

When we respect ourselves, we also learn to trust whose shoulders to cry on and whose to stand on.

Another Yes Sister helped me stop talking about past personal failures as only negative experiences and instead use them as learning tools to help me move forward. We really can convert our tough times into life lessons that work for our good.

Even in my darkest hours, when I didn't see that God was working, something inside me knew I still had value. Even while I was receiving so much input from people who claimed otherwise.

An innate understanding of our value is within all of us, possibly buried deeper than we're able to identify. God lets us know we're somebody. We're loved. Even the most horrific experiences can't destroy His quiet, personal call to us.

Ask Him for the grace to believe what He says about your value a little more than you believed Him yesterday. And ask Him for Yes Sisters who can speak into you those truths about your worth. After all, He is the one who put them in your life in the first place. God specializes in transforming what is unseen, overlooked, and viewed as unworthy to create something beautiful that transforms lives and points the world to Him.

A WORD FROM
a Yes Sister

Suzanne Eller, *author and speaker, Proverbs 31 Ministries*

Worth Discovering

Two-year-old Josiah plopped in my lap, a sticky peanut butter sandwich in one hand and goldfish crackers in the other. He snuggled close and his eyes grew heavy.

Josiah and I have a special relationship. He is always welcome in my arms. I love the feel of his dark curls against my cheek.

Yet the reality is that this little guy won't always feel safe. As he grows up, people will let him down. Circumstances and conversations will make him feel "less than." Some will judge and find him wanting. As much as I want to protect Josiah from all of that, I can't.

One day, when he is older, I will tell him this truth: *our worth will never be found in people.*

When people are the measuring stick of our value, we go up and down emotionally like a roller coaster. We are "up" when someone says or does something nice or affirming. We tumble down when they are unkind, unjust, or disparaging.

Jesus gave his disciples these simple commandments: "Love the Lord your God with all your heart and with all your soul and with all your mind" (Matt. 22:37) and "As I have loved you, so you must love one another" (John 13:34).

In these commandments, we find our worth.

For when we love the Lord our God with all our hearts, we discover whose we are. He becomes a safe place that cannot be shaken. He never changes. He is with us always. His words are truth and trustworthy.

When we follow Jesus's command to love people as God loves us, we begin to see them through His eyes. They may be messy. They may be a work in progress. However, the more we recognize their value to God, the more we see our own.

As I held my sweet grandson in my arms, it was with the realization that there will always be people who say or do hurtful things—whether to my grandson, to me, or to you.

Yet when we build our foundation on a relationship with God and choose to love others as he loves us, the impact of these people's hurtful words and actions is not the same.

People matter, but they are not the measure of our worth.

Some words and actions will sting, but they don't define us. Words of affirmation and accolades are nice, but that's not what drives us.

Instead, we plop down in the presence of our Heavenly Father, where we are always welcome, always loved, and always safe.

Then we get up and love others the same way.

Chapter 6

We CAN Find People to Love Us

A new commandment I give to you, that you love one another: just as I have loved you, you also are to love one another.

John 13:34 ESV

Two bare lightbulbs hung from cords that jutted down from the water-stained ceiling. Their lazy illumination gave the visitor the impression that even inanimate objects were there reluctantly. Either that, or the bulbs hesitated to reveal the room's conditions.

Tara lingered in the doorway. Part of her wanted to retreat and catch the next plane back across the globe. But the part of her that won out knew she was meant to make this visit.

She'd already met the child she was sponsoring in a nearby village. But after hearing about this place from one of the sponsor-center workers, she'd felt compelled to make this side trip.

Around the room, mildew decorated the chipped plaster walls. A layer of old dirt attempted to hide the floor's age. Cloying humidity intensified the rankness of soiled diapers. As much as it left to be desired, the room was the only "home" these little ones had known.

Rows of baby cribs filled the space. Each bed contained at least one young child, two if they were the smallest infants. None of the children stood to greet her. All she saw were flashes of a hand, the dark crown of a head, a corner of a thin blanket.

And the only sounds were the hum of a fan and the echo of lonely quiet. So many children but no chatter. How was that possible?

Three women, all dressed in simple cotton uniforms, observed her from behind two tables cluttered with cloths and bottles.

Guilt settled on her. She was an intruder witnessing this.

The oldest caretaker shyly approached, and Tara reached out in greeting. The woman bowed slightly, then backed away as if relinquishing her workspace once again to Western eyes.

Left on her own, Tara made her way between the closest rows of cribs. The children's names and general statistics were posted on the bed rails, but Tara couldn't read the foreign script.

The first few children appeared to be toddlers. Some slept, but others looked up at her. She paused to smile at each one, frequently reaching down to brush a wisp of hair from a pale brow.

None of the children responded with more than a blink. The majority were missing teeth. Not a roll of baby pudge was to be seen.

Tara swallowed. The basic information she'd been given before coming to the orphanage had not prepared her for the void in the room. None of these children engaged with her. She'd never seen such blank expressions, and not only from a few of them.

Steeling herself, she determined to give attention to each child before she left.

With renewed purpose, she continued. Most of the boys and girls looked younger than they probably were. Not a single one thrived. In a short time, life had withered them.

Toward the end of the last row, Tara saw her. A dark-haired girl Tara guessed to be about three years old sat up in her crib. Her black eyes were trained on the stranger heading her way.

As Tara neared the bars of her crib, the girl waved unsteady arms.

"Hello there." Tara wrapped the girl's small hand in her own.

The girl's thin, stained shirt was big enough to cover her knees. She opened her mouth like she was attempting a smile.

Tara smiled back, mute as the child seemed to be.

The girl swayed and let out an awkward grunt.

"Oh, so you are a talkative one." Tara lifted the child easily and held her close. She searched the crib's identity card for the child's name.

"Ana."

Tara turned. The elderly caretaker nodded. "Ana," she repeated.

"Well, it's very nice to meet you, Ana. My mother's name was Anna."

A slip of drool escaped Ana's open mouth.

With the cuff of her long sleeve, Tara wiped Ana's face. She kissed the girl's small forehead, gave her another gentle squeeze, and then returned her to the crib.

Days later, Tara parked her Honda in the garage. Still adjusting to jet lag from the flight home, she'd taken the day to catch up on grocery shopping and bills. It was her ex-husband's weekend with their two teenagers, so she faced an evening by herself. After fixing a bowl of cereal, she settled on her couch to watch television.

An hour later, she gave up trying to find a show that held her attention. She went to the kitchen to heat the teakettle. Minutes later, she turned off the lights in the house and carried a steaming mug to the back porch.

Stars speckled the summer night sky. Moonlight glowed over the neighbors' yards that backed up to her own.

Lights from each home hinted at what the families inside were doing. A shade lowered on the second floor of one house, where parents were probably readying their littles for bed.

The home directly behind hers was completely lit.

The Jacobsens. With six kids, their house always buzzed with activity.

Tara sighed, missing the liveliness her own household used to know. She saw less and less of her kids these days. Barrett was dating a girl who lived near Tara's ex, so he wanted to stay with his father more and more often. And Celia's schedule was always overbooked with track practices and her job at the mall. They weren't fazed when Tara left for the trip overseas. They'd had supper together only once since she'd returned.

She leaned back in her wicker chair and looked around the porch. She could read a book. Or maybe work on a crossword.

The three other chairs on the porch sat vacant, looking as if they were waiting for friends to fill them.

Tara sipped her tea and thought of the children in the orphanage. Ana's sweet face filled her memory, and she wished she could do something to help the little girl. Her wistful sigh sounded loud in the dark night.

Near or far, young or old, privileged or lacking. It didn't matter. Loneliness was no respecter of persons.

It could find anyone.

● ● ●

Even if we're surrounded by neighbors, coworkers, fellow commuters, or people at the grocery store, life can still whisper that we are alone. Or, even worse, that no one cares to find us.

I've been there. You've been there.

Some of my loneliest years happened in the middle of my marriage and my raising children. Although my home and my days were full, the list of people who looked into my heart seemed short.

Anytime we feel overlooked or invisible or unworthy of being noticed, it's tempting to doubt how much we're loved. The world is filled with lonely people. Some have *never* experienced the power of love. It's tragic.

But God created love, and love in action is the antidote to loneliness. He knows how to bring love into each of our lives.

And there's more hope. As Tara would soon discover, each of us plays a role in curing the epidemic of the "overlooked and underloved."

When Tara couldn't even process that it was love she needed most, God saw her and brought a Yes Sister to her. And that was just the beginning.

I started to see positive change as He brought one Yes Sister after another my way, and as I responded with steps of faith. God often uses Yes Sisters to show us that it's possible to find people to love us—and whom we can love. I know this from experience.

My mother is one of those people for me, a constant in my ups and downs. When depression had broken my spirit, she welcomed my children and me back home. She's always offered her encouragement and her protection as she was best able. Her presence and attention have consistently dispelled some of my feelings of loneliness and unworthiness.

My friend Maurita is another one of those people. A straight shooter and one of the most loyal people I've known, she has been there for me at my lowest. Maurita's that one girlfriend every woman needs. Outspoken and never pulling any punches, she tells it like it is. "Girl, you aren't giving up. We've got things to do. You can do this." I can't quit when Maurita's around, and I'm so grateful.

Vetta Cash is a third woman whose presence dispels loneliness for me. She's a pastor's wife and an advocate for mental health awareness at her church. She works with women to help them live their best lives. I asked Vetta to speak at my first women's conference, and she responded with delight. The conference proved challenging and left me wondering what my next steps were, professionally and personally. Vetta didn't judge me for my struggles but encouraged me by validating my worth. Her loving friendship is a great blessing that keeps me going.

My daughter, Chantel, has been another precious Yes Sister in my life. She is a beautiful young woman who amazes me with her innate expectation of more from life and love. She's so different from how I was at her age. She inspires me not to settle for an unfilled heart. And she has always seen into my emotions, even filling in for me at home when my schedule was crazy and I couldn't keep up.

Chantel was a great one for keeping things functioning, making sure neither of her brothers wore mismatched clothes when they walked out of the house. She made me so proud during the chaotic days leading up to my third women's conference. Stepping in with savvy assertiveness beyond her years, Chantel was my right-hand girl, ensuring that every detail of the conference was addressed as she knew I'd want it to be.

These women and others model love in action and refuse to let me go unnoticed. I'm safe with each of them.

They give me a picture of God's attentive love. His love deepens our security, and our self-worth grows healthier. We develop a courageous lifestyle rather than a resigned existence.

I'm living proof. I wasn't born bold. Somehow my daughter got the *chutzpah*, but not me! Unshakable courage and self-worth are not part of my natural temperament. But I'm growing as I experience love. And, God bless them, my Yes Sisters are partly to blame.

Love feeds our whole being. It heals us and draws us to full life.

It's true that much can be said for living content and grateful lives. But on the deepest spiritual level, we're made to be *unsatisfiable* with halfway living. That is, if love is the half we're missing. This explains why unloved children wither in every way: physically, spiritually, emotionally, intellectually, socially.

The angst we experience from halfway living, missing real love, serves a mighty purpose. It helps us recognize our need for God, the only one who can fill us completely.

Like Chantel, Yes Sisters most definitely can be younger women. A younger Yes Sister might live next door or work in the adjoining cubicle. She may sit next to you in a continuing education class or ask you every few weeks how you're doing while you sit in her salon chair and get her opinion about a new hairstyle. The world is wide open to Yes Sister discoveries, even if these sisters are many years younger than you.

But often our sisters have started ahead of us on this path of discovery. Their lives illuminate love's effects. They often can understand our struggle, because they've been through tough seasons. They have felt the love and healing of other sisters, and most importantly, of Jesus.

Love is alive, and it's contagious. It can't keep to itself. No heart can remain stagnant forever in its presence. Love's propensity to reach out is closely linked to its complementary characteristics of care, forgiveness, grace, truth, and unselfishness.

Love wants others to discover how it can, how it *will*, change lives. As I continue to find wholeness in Jesus, my passion keeps me looking for ways to offer His love and hope to more women.

I pray you have at least one Yes Sister in your story who has modeled becoming secure in love. But if you don't, there is hope for you. The world is big and loaded with opportunities. What do we do when we feel alone? How do we find others to love us and others we can love?

How do we find Yes Sisters?

Let's return to Tara's story.

A WORD FROM
a Yes Sister

Barb Roose, *speaker and author*

My Pink Circle of Yes Sisters

As a full-time speaker and author, my life is a series of learning curves. Unlike previously when my jobs came with biweekly paychecks, employer health insurance, and a handy dental plan, my life now is a daily walk-by-faith adventure. God has surrounded me with a group of trusted voices to support me and cheer me on along the way. Angelia White calls her group Yes Sisters. I call this group of women my *Pink Circle*. Here's what my circle looks like:

Mentor Friend—The fellow speaker/author who has more experience and lets me ask lots of questions.

Adventurous Friend—This friend is a constant source of "Yes, you can!" encouragement.

Cautious Friend—This friend elevates the drawbacks, flip sides, or worst-case scenarios, which helps my go-go-go feet stay on the ground.

Praying Friend—This friend doesn't give a lot of advice, but she prays mightily on my behalf.

Secret Friend—She knows my deepest secrets, worst mistakes, and biggest dreams, so she helps me keep a healthy perspective.

While we never meet as a group, I talk to them individually at least once a month, if not several times a month. These women have permission to raise red flags when they are concerned about my health or spiritual wellness. They have permission to encourage me to say no to whatever isn't God's best for me.

My circle of trusted confidantes grew out of relationships developed over the years while participating in small group Bible studies or volunteering at church. We started talking over cups of tea and coffee. We shared our lives with each other.

Over the years, these beautiful women have walked with me as I've encountered challenging career transitions, celebrated new book contracts, and handled catastrophic family crises. I am in solo ministry, but I'm grateful that I never have to face life's ups and downs alone.

Chapter 7

We CAN Find Yes Sisters

One who has unreliable friends soon comes to ruin,
but there is a friend who sticks closer than a brother
[or sister!].

Proverbs 18:24

Tara had a rough few years leading up to her visit to the overseas orphanage. After her divorce, she moved to a smaller home in a town where she didn't know anyone. She had to get a new job that paid more money. But the new office atmosphere encouraged competition more than camaraderie, and she missed her old work friends.

Grieving her marriage and all the changes that divorce brought prompted Tara to look for fresh hope. More time alone got her thinking about what she wanted to do with her life.

When a speaker at church invited the congregation to sponsor children in need overseas, she jumped at the opportunity. Helping someone else, especially a needy child, brought hope to her lonely heart. Within a couple of days, a picture of six-year-old Claudia hung on Tara's refrigerator.

That was four years ago. It had taken Tara that long to scrape together enough money to visit Claudia. Little did Tara know how God had been working behind the scenes—in the middle of her own heartache—for a greater purpose.

In the weeks following her trip to meet Claudia and Ana, she couldn't get either girl off her mind. It had been so good to see Claudia thriving and laughing and playing with her family, the mission workers, and the other children.

But what about Ana? What about the many children wasting away without love or affection or any of the opportunities Tara had enjoyed much of her life?

She could do something more. She knew it.

One day she was walking in her neighborhood with her new puppy, Sherman. When she passed the Jacobsens' home, she waved to Nadine Jacobsen, who was watering flowers on the porch. Nadine set down the watering can and invited Tara in for lemonade.

The welcoming gesture began a friendship that quickly deepened. Tara appreciated Nadine's gracious, forthright nature. One day over lunch, Tara nervously shared the idea that had been keeping her up at night.

To Tara's relief, Nadine's face shone.

"You've got to do something with this." Nadine set down her fork and leaned closer. "How can I help?"

With lots of prayer and guidance, Tara took one step of faith after another. She worked with the organization through which she supported Claudia to establish a fund for the orphanage.

Tara faced challenges, but God responded with provision after provision, reinforcing Tara's belief that her vision was from Him. When doubts plagued her, she depended on Nadine for a boost to keep going.

And one of Claudia's teachers, Mae Lin, jumped on board with Tara's vision. She'd been praying for a way to offer practical hope to more local children who didn't have sponsors. Tara and Mae Lin became strong Yes Sisters for each other, despite speaking different languages and living a world apart.

Generous donations provided a better facility for the orphanage, more caretakers and training for them, health care and therapy for the children, an onsite nutritionist, and even a safe outdoor space so the kids could benefit from fresh air and physical activities.

Ana bloomed far beyond what Tara had hoped for. Twenty years later, the once-mute little girl with a malnourished body and soul returned to the orphanage. Ana had finished college and came home to fill an assistant therapist position. She wanted to offer children the love and resources that had turned her life around. The onsite doctor, Claudia, recommended her for the job.

Tara had retired by then. She used her savings and free time to visit Ana, Claudia, and Mae Lin on a regular basis. Nadine occasionally made the trip with her, and Tara's children joined her once a year.

Ask, Seek, Knock

Yes Sisters can change the world for others. When we trace the events of our lives, we see how God uses everyday actions from everyday people to transform everyday lives into something extraordinary.

Ana might have died alone and unloved in that broken-down orphanage crib if it hadn't been for a woman with an aching heart, a new puppy that needed exercise, an offer of lemonade, and a new friend—a Yes Sister who encouraged a lonely woman to take a courageous step of faith.

Neither Nadine nor Tara thought of Ana as needing a Yes Sister, but their story illustrates that God uses Yes Sisters to do His work even in the lives of little girls. A Yes Sister's impact transcends geography and generations.

Tara's ongoing care of Ana helped Ana learn to be a Yes Sister. And so the legacy continues.

● ● ●

Tara and Ana are fictional characters, but their stories are drawn from real experiences, real emotions, real need. They could be any of us.

Young and old, we're all part of God's worldwide network of sisters. He's been growing this sisterhood ever since the second girl joined Eve on the earth. That's a long time, and He's a pro at connecting us.

But the world is big. How do we find women who can be more than acquaintances or casual friends, women who can be our Yes Sisters?

And how can we discover our own unique way to be a Yes Sister to someone else?

Matthew 7:7–8 says, "Ask and it will be given to you; seek and you will find; knock and the door will be opened to you. For everyone who asks receives; the one who seeks finds; and to the one who knocks, the door will be opened."

These Scriptures apply to so many areas of our lives, including finding and being Yes Sisters. When we follow the ask, seek, and knock portion of these verses, the second portion is a promise: those who ask *will* receive, those who seek *will* find, and to those who knock, the door *will* be opened.

Ask

Start by relying on the Lord first and foremost. Ask God to bring you true and meaningful friendships. There's no substitute for what He will bring you.

Because he formed the need inside of us, God knows we have to have friendships with other women. He created us to be greater through friendships. So ask away! And when you ask, believe that God is bringing Yes Sisters into your life, from anywhere in the world.

Ask also applies when you meet a woman in whom you sense a kindred or a mentor spirit. If you admire a quality about her— grace under fire, tenacity despite disappointment, joy in the day to day—by all means, affirm her for it. In time, you may see an opportunity to ask her how she learned to live so positively.

Seek

After you ask God for Yes Sisters, don't just wait around for them to show up. Faith means action. Go look for friendships, or at least go to the places they may be found. Initiating relationships will feel more natural each time you reach out to someone in friendship.

Many of my Yes Sisters didn't live in my neighborhood or go to the church I was attending at the time. To get to the next season in my life, I had to listen when God said, "Move." When I did, God was able to bring new friendships into my life.

Yes Sisters may be waiting for you in organized clubs, in gatherings of women with similar interests and passions, in your career, around your neighborhood, or among the women you meet in your role as a wife or mom.

If you enjoy quilting or painting with watercolor or fishing or hiking, look for groups in your area that share your interests. If you are starting a business or already running one, attend meetings at your local chamber of commerce or join local or regional business-women organizations.

If you're a mom, look for groups that have Bible studies or stroller exercise excursions. Writers groups, gardening co-ops, baking clubs, volunteer opportunities, ministries . . . the list could go on and on.

Look where your interests are, and most likely, you'll find your people.

You can recognize a Yes Sister by her character. She stands out like gold for one reason or many. Here are a few clues: She is honest, fun, encouraging, trustworthy, appreciative, and a genuine confidante. She is tender with your past, present in your present, and hopeful for your future.

She models humility when she messes up and forgiveness when you do. She might push you at times when all you want to do is push back. But she's solid in her motivations no matter what. She's beautifully imperfect and all the more lovable for it.

On the flip side, some traits never jibe with the character of a Yes Sister. A woman who seems to take subtle (or obvious) joy in besting you or gossips about you or anyone else doesn't show quality character. If she's too proud to own her mistakes or is driven to prove her point, you'll want to keep your heart a gracious distance away. And if someone appears only to want to teach or steer or insist that you listen to her—without appreciating what she can learn from you as well—she could use some space to grow before being trusted as a Yes Sister.

A Yes Sister reminds you that small things *do* matter, so celebrate them. She could have earned her degree in prayer partnering, with minors in loving, nurturing, positivity, and faithfulness.

And as both the cornerstone of her identity and the cherry on the top—she seeks to grow more like her Savior every year. Watching her life inspires you toward the same priority.

She's out there, maybe closer than you imagine. You can find her!

If you've come across a woman like this, take her smile as encouragement to get to know her. Openness, friendliness, efforts to get to know you for you, thoughtful questions and responses, not seeking attention for herself, and a good friendship track record others can vouch for are signs that it's okay to reach out to her.

I have found my Yes Sisters in all kinds of places.

When I began *HOPE for Women* magazine, I started connecting with other women online: bloggers, writers, businesswomen, and other dreamers. I found many of my Yes Sisters through those connections. Some of them were long-ago friends with whom I reconnected. Some I didn't meet in person for many years. Some I still have never met face-to-face.

In this technology age, we don't have to share a city or even a continent to have community. I met my friend Sherrell Jenkins online through *HOPE*. She is a subscriber who took the initiative to encourage me in my work. She's always supportive, sending notes and inbox messages to say she appreciates all that the team is doing with the magazine. After we'd connected that way for a while, she even sent flowers with a note to say she was proud of me. God sends her to me at the right times.

Initiating friendship can feel intimidating, especially if you've been burned. One way to get past any misgivings is to focus on simply being friendly. Friendliness doesn't cost anything, but it can lift your spirits. It offers a gift of kindness to another person that will bless both her and you.

So go out and seek!

Knock

If you feel an inner connection with another woman, you could be surprised when she takes the next steps. But if she doesn't, don't let the connection go. Don't walk away and hope she will keep in touch. Don't wait for something more to happen. You'll never know what amazing things were behind that door you turned away from. Take a bold step.

Knocking means doing the next step after seeking. It's time to be proactive and consider what next step you need to take to develop something meaningful. Set a coffee date, send a follow-up note, invite her for a walk or an event, drop off a meal. Do something.

Knocking takes time. It's added effort. It could mean *not* knocking on other doors. It takes discernment to know which friendships to pursue, and that takes us back to prayer and asking God.

You are part of something huge, this sisterhood. You received your invitation when you were born. God's plans for your role are worlds bigger than you can dream. So imagine.

He will connect you with your Yes Sisters.

Right now, women are out there longing to find you as much as you long to find them. Ask, seek, knock, and you'll discover who they are.

That kind of active faith gets us started. It's also what keeps us going.

A WORD FROM
a Yes Sister

Holley Gerth, *bestselling author of* Fiercehearted

Better Together

Last night a group of women gathered in my home. We're all writers and we come together to cheer each other on, pray for each other, and of course, eat good snacks. As I looked around my living room, I felt astonished and humbled that these women would choose to share life and ministry with me.

I thought back to when the group began and how scared I felt about it. I'd been feeling lonely as a writer and I longed for sisters who understood. I kept looking for community with a creative tribe in my area but couldn't quite find it. At some point, I realized that perhaps God was asking me to make it.

This seemed like an intimidating prospect. It would mean saying yes to many things that made me uncomfortable.

Yes to getting to know new women and the inevitable awkwardness that entails.

Yes to opening the door of my home when I don't consider hospitality a strength of mine.

Yes to choosing to open my heart, too, when as an introvert it would be easier not to.

I took a deep breath and plunged ahead. The group began with a handful of women and now has grown to almost thirty. Not all of us can make it every month, but I'm grateful for everyone who can, who decides to say their own courageous yes too.

As we talked last night, I thought of how I'm now hearing and saying yes in a different way. Those first fears are gone. Now yes sounds like saying to each other . . .

"Yes, you can write that book God has put on your heart."

"Yes, you can accept that speaking engagement even though you're scared."

"Yes, you're making a difference—don't quit."

Not everyone needs a group of writers. Someone else might need to connect with other moms or coworkers, artists or accountants. In our group, we say, "We all need to find people who are the same kind of weird as we are." And I would say to any woman who's afraid of community with other women that you can take heart in knowing that the yeses required get easier. It's the initial ones that can trip us up, hold us back, and keep us alone.

Dare to reach out. Dare to take the risk. Dare to say yes to letting others into your life. None of us needs to have it all together. We all just need to remember we're better together.

Chapter 8

Our Faith WILL Sustain Us

Thus says the Lord,
   your Redeemer, the Holy One of Israel:
"I am the Lord your God,
   who teaches you to profit,
   who leads you in the way you should go."

Isaiah 48:17 ESV

At times, my faith has felt shoestring thin. I've doubted God was enough.

During my twenties and thirties, scarcity was the only abundance I knew. That, and shame that came from chronically doing without.

I was caught in a tornado I couldn't escape.

My marriage had always been one of "yours or mine," not "ours." The income I earned from various jobs went to paying bills. Groceries and most of our children's needs came out of my paychecks, leaving little to nothing for fun and dreaming. I grieved not having resources to do more for my kids. Relying on my parents well into adulthood was not the way I'd envisioned life.

There they were again: the nos.

No money.

No acceptance of who I was, who I am.

No filling of my heart.

No room to dream.

No freedom from judgment.

No respite from discouragement.

No productive faith.

No hope.

The nos rattled me. For years I was stuck. Opportunities eluded me that might have made a difference in my life or improved the condition of my heart.

Any goal I had remained outside the whirlwind. If I tried to catch a glimpse of what could be, the winds of life would sweep me into their vortex again.

Even after I began the magazine, I battled the feeling of being stuck. Nothing on my résumé relayed confidence that I was capable of developing a magazine or running the business side of it. I battled feelings of failure because of meager funds and lack of other resources. My naïveté left me vulnerable to self-serving individuals.

Then came the day that threatened to end my young venture altogether.

Soon after sending the winter and spring issues of *HOPE* to be distributed to bookstores, I received a letter from the distributing house telling me they'd filed for bankruptcy. Many businesses were struggling from a lagging economy. I'd been counting on the profits from the sales of those issues to keep the magazine running.

To make matters worse, instead of honoring our agreed-on 60/40 split of newsstand sales, the distributing house didn't sell any of the magazines. Without warning me, they threw away all the copies I'd sent to them. I didn't see a penny.

And I couldn't afford editorial help at that point to keep the online magazine profitable.

I was barely holding on. What was the good of this great dream to empower women with hope if I didn't have (1) the means to do it or (2) the know-how to get to the root of the problems that kept me in the tornado?

God, what in the world? How can I do all this? I thought.

I think back to that time and still cringe. My faith had some growing to do.

What is faith, really? Hebrews 11:1 says, "Faith is confidence in what we hope for and assurance about what we do not see."

I needed confidence and assurance, quickly. When fears nearly consumed me, I learned to start talking to God more. About everything.

"Okay, God, I'm broke," I began. "I need some help here."

Such a simple beginning, but so key. God wanted my tattered faith. He wants yours too.

Instead of beating ourselves up for not trusting Him more, we need to see that the very act of admitting our need for Him reveals our trust. Something in us knows we need Him first and foremost. That something is faith.

Answers didn't always come quickly, but through delays, setbacks, and timely victories, the belief that God would bring to fruition the dream He'd instilled in me stretched its roots deeper in my heart. After all, my dream was actually His dream.

God was working bigger things in me than merely blessing me with an income source and the chance to run my own business. It wasn't even about the financial picture. He was breaking down the nos in me to prepare me for the yeses He had in store.

Once again, He sent Yes Sisters my way.

My Yes Sister Sonya is a tough cookie, and she's an answer to prayer. I know God had her in mind when I prayed for lots of friends as a young girl.

An editor who works for me connected us. Through Sonya, I've grown in business acumen and professionalism. She possesses a knack for giving practical pointers about etiquette and other life skills while never making me feel ashamed about not knowing certain things or not being at her economic or social level. She helps me feel comfortable and confident in owning and telling my story. She's such a gift that way.

But she's more. She has also opened my spiritual ears and taught me to listen for God's voice.

"God always shows you a sign if people's motives are off and if they're just looking for an opportunity from you," she says. While urging me to trust God for discernment regarding people, Sonya encourages me to trust God, *period*.

As we practice looking to the Lord, He grows our experience of His faithfulness. Again and again, He proves that His grace sustains, supports, and lifts us.

Without the struggles, I wouldn't have learned these lessons or gone deeper in my relationship with Him.

When I asked God to reveal the beginning and the end goal of this magazine publishing assignment He's given me, I wish He would have shown me (warned me about) the tough middle spots. But then again, had I known the challenges that were coming, I probably wouldn't have started *HOPE for Women*!

Now I give every need to Him, and He always comes through.

Each of us has a purpose from Him for which we have not been given the resources to tackle on our own. He gets the glory for doing the impossible when the way seems dark to our human eyes.

I can look now and see what a girl from Muncie, Indiana, with a big dream and no journalism or other related experience can do when God directs the path. All this has been God's craftsmanship. He is the master brander.

He is growing your faith, too, right here and now, in the circumstances that make you smile, and maybe even more so in the ones that bring you to tears. Be intentional about going to God with the issues that stretch your faith. He certainly is intentional about how He wants to use those issues for good.

Trust that God knows about anything that may hold you back. Put your heart in His hands more deeply than ever and ask Him to speak into your hurt. That thing that feels as if it's taking you down—that is the very thing He is going to use for your healing and the healing of others. The faith you gain from moving closer to God with your questions is something He will use as you become a Yes Sister for someone else.

Faith often grows up in the least likely places and from the least likely sources. That is why we hope, no matter what. Trust more deeply than you have before. Faith is the beginning of the next new.

Second Corinthians 5:7 says, "For we walk by faith, not by sight" (KJV). Some seasons require us to live out our faith in very real ways. Our plans may not make sense, but we know in the stillness and quiet of our hearts that it's the direction to go.

Our Yes Sisters help cast away the doubts that will certainly attack. Our sisters will say, "You can and will do this!" Lean on that. Trust them, and trust God. Go to God again and again, and soak in the words He speaks through your Yes Sisters.

And let faith carry you.

A WORD FROM
a Yes Sister

Liz Curtis Higgs, *bestselling author and speaker*

Trusting God through the Storm

When my doctor said, "It's cancer," I pulled out my calendar and showed her all the upcoming events at which I was scheduled to speak that fall. Chemotherapy? Radiation? Ain't nobody got time for that.

She shook her head. "You'll have to make time, Liz. Every third Monday."

Determined not to let cancer rob my joy or steal more of my time than necessary, I dutifully spent six Mondays from September to December at the cancer center and made all but two of my speaking engagements. Because that's what Yes Sisters do, right? We show up. If our hair falls out, we buy a wig and keep going.

Then came January. The last round of chemo. My heart and mind were still focused on keeping my commitments, but my body was no longer cooperating. Various side effects had taken their toll, and a deep exhaustion had settled in. Even so, I flew off to speak, pleading with the Lord to give me enough strength to make it through.

That night I sat in the front pew, staring at the platform, wondering how in the world I was going to stand to my feet, let alone walk up several steps, let alone speak for forty minutes. Silent prayers beat loud inside my heart. *Please, Lord. Please help.*

With some effort, I stood and slowly made my way to the podium, feeling desperate. *Lord, I can't do this. I can't!* His response was immediate: *you can.*

Forty minutes later, I took my seat again, stunned at what had happened. So much *energy*. So much *passion*. Who else but God could have made that possible?

In my heart, I thanked Him over and over again, confessing, *Lord, that was one hundred percent You and zero percent me!*

Then He gently corrected me, and I learned the truth. *Liz, it's always been that way. Always.*

PART 2

Yes in Action

Chapter 9

We CAN Create Our Dreams

> I can do everything through Christ, who gives me strength.
>
> Philippians 4:13 NLT

The opening paragraph of Bruce Wilkinson's book *The Dream Giver* connected with my soul and pushed hope straight into my core.

> Not long ago and not far away, a Nobody named Ordinary lived in the Land of Familiar. Every day was pretty much the same for Ordinary. . . . Until the day Ordinary noticed a small, nagging feeling that something big was missing from his life. . . . And even though Nobodies in Familiar didn't generally expect the unexpected, Ordinary began to wish for it.[1]

I was Ordinary! And I'd had enough of it.

I'd been existing but not really living. Resigned to less than God's best for me. Missing the truth that He had wanted to fill me all along. But He was about to change all that. He would begin by changing me from the inside.

The Misconception of Contentment

How easily our busy days lull us into mistaking resignation for contentment. We're taught not to be complainers—everyone has problems, right? So we chastise ourselves if satisfaction in life remains elusive. Maybe we subconsciously view any dissatisfaction as selfish or wrong.

A misconception about true contentment can lock us in guilt and fool us into neglecting what we know God intends to use to fill our hearts.

We, as women, are especially sensitive to the needs of others but too often deny our own needs. We see to others first and second and third, until our spirits gasp for life-breath. *And then we still keep going!*

Full days do not necessarily mean full lives. Need-meeters who neglect their own needs starve and exhaust themselves until they become too weak to serve or too resentful to serve well.

God's compassionate plan is for us to sacrifice ourselves for the needs of others, which is a reflection of His sacrificial love. But we miss the mark if we sacrifice to the point of self-destruction. We, too, are needy. Finding what makes us stronger and fulfilled and seeing to our own needs makes us better people who are then better able to serve well.

That thought runs contrary to the nurturing nature of many women. We forget to nurture, protect, and grow ourselves.

I know a woman—Kelly—who pushed aside an issue in her marriage that tangled her emotions far too long. Her struggle had to do with her husband's volunteer work. He committed a great deal of time to a ministry that reached out to parolees who were working to rebuild their lives.

She respected the way her husband cared for those former inmates. They needed help, and he was there for them. Four mornings and three evenings a week, he was there for them. And on his free nights, he focused on their children.

But Kelly needed him too. Their relationship needed his presence. Their connection was weakening, and they were no longer a thriving model of God's design for unity in marriage.

She fought her growing resentment about not feeling like a priority in her husband's schedule—or in his heart. And the thought that she was being demanding or selfish riddled her with guilt.

Years inched by while she burdened herself with more self-condemnation. She'd listen to her self-shaming inner voice that said Christians are supposed to put others first. How could she have a problem with all the sacrifices her husband made to help others? And their children? She thought—and was told—she wasn't godly enough to get past the problem.

She continued to ignore how much the imbalance of her husband's priorities was taking from her. She told herself she needed to pray more, to release more. That she was too selfish to get over the hurt.

Finally, Kelly realized she was starving emotionally in her marriage. She sought the listening ears of several Yes Sisters who helped her sort through her feelings and encouraged her to seek professional counseling. She did critical business in prayer with God about His truths related to her needs and emotions.

Instead of hearing God demand that she work harder to accept the situation, she felt His strong, quiet voice urging her to *not* accept it. To speak up. To stop a pattern that was destructive to her well-being and her marriage. His grace and assurance validated her. She understood for the first time that God never wanted her to remain passive and content with her husband's failure to invest in their relationship. What she felt was never true contentment anyway but instead was a misconception that had really messed with her.

God wasn't condemning her for her discontent or lack of gratitude. He was working all along, through that very discontent she'd condemned, to highlight a trouble spot in her marriage that needed tending.

Her needs mattered to the Lord. They needed to matter to her too—for her well-being, her marriage, and God's bigger work in her life.

Her needs needed to matter so her husband could grow in ways he'd neglected. And they needed to matter so her children could observe a healthy, balanced mother who respects herself. She began to share more honestly with her husband about how she was feeling. As a result, he began to better understand her and his responsibility to prioritize their marriage and home life.

God never intended for Kelly to be falsely satisfied with less than what He desires for her. Today she is healing from the emotional suffocation and growing in strength, joy, and hope. She is now better able to be her own daughter's Yes Sister by modeling how to live as a fully equipped woman of God. A woman who has experienced God's grace and truth.

The Bible does not teach us to love the dullness that comes from living without expecting God's yes. It does, however, teach that we find contentment, through both the blessings and the hard times, squarely in God's good plan for us.

A Problem with Gratitude?

Gratitude is another concept we use to avoid any feelings of unfulfillment. We hear much about how increasing our thankfulness increases our joy. Yes, a gratitude attitude can transform our ability to be content.

However . . . (This is a life-altering *however* for some of us.)

Not all discontent means we aren't thankful enough. Not all discontent reveals a character flaw or spiritual problem. Instead, the drive to improve or correct what isn't working is often fueled by need or something higher—God's design. This distinction has taken me a long time to embrace. If the lack of a stop sign on the corner of Third and Main has been at least partially responsible for several recent accidents—including a fatality—no town official worth their salt would respond to complaints by arguing, "The town has lots of other stop signs. Why can't you be content? Aren't you grateful for what the town has already installed?"

In some cases, we are motivated to precipitate a change because it's the right thing to do, not because we lack gratitude or are discontent.

When God speaks yes to us, His yes comes with a permission slip. Really, it's more than permission. It's an invitation to a kind of dissatisfaction that is not related to ingratitude at all. Instead, it's a laser-targeted discontent or restlessness God plants within us for the purpose of motivating us to walk with Him into something new.

We can be grateful and content in Him all day long. But those disciplines are not intended to overshadow or extinguish God's purposeful stirring within us when His dream for us is at stake. We can be grateful for that kind of discontent. Some of the most impactful inventions and technological innovations have been born out of being discontent with present systems.

Trusted sisters who draw their counsel from God and have our best interests at heart can offer direction when we're tempted to use *discontent* and *ingratitude* in ways they weren't intended.

Bruce Wilkinson's Ordinary had to learn to listen for the Dream Giver's voice each step of his journey. Like us, he had many questions along the way. But as Ordinary moved and rested in faith again and again, he learned to know and trust the Dream Giver's character and love for him. And one by one, his doubts and questions fell behind him.

Two "Cans"

"The Dream Giver gave me a Big Dream! I was made to be a Some-body and destined to achieve Great Things!"[2]

The discovery of God's desires for us captivates us with hope, one of our truest needs.

When Ordinary realized that the Dream Giver wanted more for him, he felt giddy with excitement.

And then he felt these two doubts:

1. Was he enough for the dream? "Ordinary realized he had a problem. His Big Dream was *too* big for a Nobody like Ordinary."[3]

2. Would he be allowed to pursue it? All Ordinary knew of chasing dreams came from his father's remorse about his own unfulfilled dream: "'I waited for a chance to pursue it. I waited and waited. But it never seemed possible.' . . . Of all the sad words Ordinary had ever heard, these were the saddest."[4]

Believing we can create our dreams involves two "can" ques-tions. They are the same ones Ordinary faced. The can of ability asks if we are capable, and the can of permission wonders if we are allowed.

The Can of Ability

Can I accomplish my dream?

Nothing in my past or my previous work experience would have moved an employer to hire me with any amount of confidence that I could create and manage a magazine. I wouldn't have hired a stranger with my former résumé for that job either!

I can smile about that now as I watch *HOPE for Women* magazine grow and expand. But a true success story is not because of the accomplishment itself or any human being's capability.

My story speaks boldly of *God*, not me. And sometimes of God *despite* me. The more I learn to know Him, the more I want my life to reflect His life in me.

His strength in my weakness.

His courage in my timidity.

His peace in my fears.

His resources in my lack.

His grace in my failures.

His hope in my doubts.

His abundance in my scarcity.

And His yes over every one of my nos. Amen!

The can of ability speaks of the Lord's power, not our own. What He intends, He will bring to fruition. He only wants our willingness and our trust.

In her ninety-day devotional, *Awaken*, Priscilla Shirer—a woman who became an unofficial Yes Sister to me through her powerful insights—speaks to this truth with these words:

> Your God . . . will grant you the full supply you need to excel at His purposes today, no matter how varied or prodigious those tasks may be. Every decision you need to make, every task you need to accomplish, every relationship you need to navigate, every element of daily life you need to traverse, God has already perfectly matched it up with an equivalent-to-overflowing supply of His grace. And you must believe this . . . because whether or not you do will directly affect your ability to function out of this overflow in your daily life.[5]

It's the promise in 2 Corinthians 9:8: "God is able to make all grace abound to you, so that having all sufficiency in all things at all times, you may abound in every good work" (ESV).

I love the *all*-consuming coverage in that verse.

If you feel inadequate for your dream, you're in the right frame of mind for God to glorify Himself and grow your faith in His strength and goodness.

The success God desires for us does require us to work hard instead of waiting around for something to happen. However, that kind of holding pattern is very different from stillness. When God is orchestrating events, we find ourselves repeatedly surprised into a stillness of spirit as we watch Him provide, move, and complete His plans.

This is me serving as a Yes Sister for you right now: you can ably pursue your dreams because God is able.

The Can of Permission

Am I allowed to pursue my dream?

Work, family life, service, and miscellaneous activities—both important and unimportant—can leave us wishing for thirty-six-hour days.

Taking precious minutes away from our responsibilities to pursue something that fills our own heart or recharges our internal batteries can feel self-centered.

But until we take seriously God's instructions for us to keep moving toward the desires He puts on our hearts, they may remain out of our reach.

Just because our dreams have stretched far beyond our view doesn't mean God has lost sight of them. Some seasons don't allow us much time to focus on our dreams. Some seasons require our devotion to the needs of others. But even then God is at work in our hearts, preparing us for a more active time of "dream chasing" down the road, if we're listening and collecting the life experiences that will equip us.

The quiet years when a hope seems like a background whisper are not inactive ones. Critical preparation and training can happen in those seasons.

Keep listening for God's voice. Quiet seasons do not mean He isn't working in you and your situation. The gentle nudges to your spirit that keep reminding you of your dream may be God giving you permission to keep bringing it to Him and acquiring what might seem at first to be unrelated skills and background.

When appropriate, talk about your heart's desires with Yes Sisters you know will listen and pray for you, even during the holding patterns.

And put a big, open-hearted, sky's-the-limit request before the Lord. Ask Him to reveal what Ephesians 3:20 will look like in your life: "[God] . . . is able to do immeasurably more than all we ask or imagine, according to his power that is at work within us."

He loves our requests to see Him glorified. The desires He gives us are meant to point toward Him, to highlight His greatness first and foremost. He *wants* to do more in and through us than we could ever dream up on our own.

So accept His permission. Full heart. All in.

Today your pursuit of the dreams He gives you may center on steady prayerfulness or taking one step of faith. It could be asking Him to prepare you by growing your endurance and trusting in Him through a waiting period or in the face of a closed door.

He does not forget His plans for you. Right now, you have His permission—His instruction, even—to pursue the goals He gives you.

Our dreams from God will always require more than our resources can handle. They are also always for a purpose greater than ourselves. This means our pursuit of His dreams is *unselfish*, as long as we are walking in step with Him instead of rushing ahead for our own satisfaction.

If we tune our spirits to His, we'll discover what other possibilities God might be speaking. We'll hear the applause of heaven . . . and the applause of the Yes Sisters around us who are cheering us on with each baby step toward His goals for us.

Yes is the whisper of God that He has *more*. Have faith that He is guiding you, overcoming what's old and worn and hasn't been working.

Trust His beckoning. Faith is the beginning of the next new season.

● ● ●

Can you feel it—the beckon of *yes*?

> It nudges a long-quiet wonder.
> > It surprises with an awareness that you are *not* to remain
> > "content."
> Striving for more gratitude will not hush it.
> > Busying yourself will not scatter it.
> It's the swell of something new in the air,
> > the exhale that breathes,
> *It's time.*

A WORD FROM
a Yes Sister

LaTara V. Bussey, *success mindset coach, online marketing consultant, author, speaker*

Dreaming for Each Other

I can remember when I met Angie in 2005. She sent me a private message about wanting to start a newsletter for churches. As we talked on the phone and she poured out her vision, I thought she was a woman with a mission.

We talked for over an hour about her dreams. I was not sure why, but hearing them excited me. Something in her voice caused my soul to leap. I needed a soul leap at that time because I was living in a very deep depression. So much of Angie's dream helped me to dream, even when abuse told me no. Her leaps became my yes in so many ways.

What I am sharing with you now is in response to this question: "Was there a time when another woman told you that you could do your dream or a time that you told another woman she could do hers?"

Most definitely. I could barely dream when I met Angie. But she was always dreaming enough for both of us. The value in sisterhood is not that everyone always has a dream but that sometimes we must dream for our sisters. Amid the chaos and clutter of life, it can be hard to dream for ourselves.

Little did we know that the publication we were trying to bring to life would grow a sisterhood along with it. What is now *HOPE for Women* magazine began with two women holding on to faith for the chance to dream beyond our wildest imagining.

Chapter 10

We WILL Overcome

Despite all these things, overwhelming victory is ours through Christ, who loved us.

Romans 8:37 NLT

In September 2018, Hurricane Florence struck North Carolina's shore. For days beforehand, the category 4 storm surged in the Atlantic, heading toward land while meteorologists made predictions, issued warnings, and offered advice.

Fearing the Carolina coast's "storm of a lifetime," according to the National Weather Service, thousands of people stockpiled necessities and battened down the hatches. More than one million faced mandatory evacuation orders ahead of the ferocious but slow-moving tempest.

By the time Florence made landfall, she had been downgraded to a category 1 storm. But her strong winds still raged. Trees toppled and blocked roads that river swells quickly covered. Record rainfall and flooding became serious threats. Widespread power outages complicated things even more.

In at least one town, city officials tweeted instructions for residents to go to the upper stories of their homes, with assurances that rescuers were working hard to get to those who'd been trapped.

Aggravating the situation, Florence took her not-so-sweet time and crept along at three miles per hour. That's slower than most people can walk.

Flo's aftereffects created the potential for more damage. By early October of that year, the death toll had reached more than fifty. Other losses included homes, vehicles, valuable possessions, and keepsakes.

●●●

Sometimes storms tarry rather than move on. Or they pick up speed or change direction without warning and pound us again from a different angle.

We know that most of life's storms don't come by way of weather patterns. Most of them take the form of financial struggles, relationship glitches, health declines, crime, or any number of other threats.

Many of us know sisters who've lost everything, from their marriages to their homes to their livelihoods to their reputations. Others have endured a loved one's serious illness, the death of a parent, the loss of a job, multiple moves, battles with addiction, ongoing troubles with children, or an attack on someone they care about.

On top of her own multiple surgeries and financial strain, one sister had to be "Mom" to adult parents and in-laws while caring for a sibling who was losing a fight for her health.

On social media, a prayer request was recently shared for a woman battling advanced cancer and facing single parenthood after her husband was killed in a car accident.

Yet another sister of mine is living with several chronic illnesses—more than one of them life-threatening—that require dozens of pills twice a day.

When a string of storms hit, we glance uneasily at the sky, anticipating the next lightning bolt. Extra stress on our emotions is collateral damage of the actual crises. It messes with our equilibrium, causing us to lose sight of any focal point that helps us maintain balance and steadiness.

Survival during these times can be overwhelming. How can we be expected to overcome?

What happens to our dreams when we're caught up in a storm? Is it worth continuing to expect God's best for us when so much has been taken away, leveled, destroyed?

Coming to understand from a heavenly perspective how storms deepen our roots in the Lord helps us endure. No squalls are wasted in God's weather system.

The riches we glean during these times may only be found in a storm. We learn to quiet ourselves so God's strength can refresh us. We discover the blessing of receiving, with a vulnerability that has nothing to do with weakness. And we're forever changed by God's perfect timing and provision as He sends Yes Sisters our way when we need them most.

Stay Still

My colleague's Yes Sister once shared synonyms she came across in a study of the word *endure*. To her surprise, the list included the words *stay*, *remain*, *rest*, and *be*.

Those words seem so sedentary. Words like *staying*, *remaining*, *resting*, or simply *being* imply inactivity, which is not helpful when it comes to surviving a storm. Enduring—or overcoming—suggests action, doesn't it? Aren't we supposed to be proactive, strong women who tackle tempests head-on?

As this Yes Sister considered those words, she began to understand the purposeful power of rest, of simply *being*, in the midst of any battle. Being the thoughtful woman she is, she shared what she'd unearthed. It's a privilege to share it now with you.

In a storm, God shows us where to find our real strength. It is always found in Him. And we can only hear Him if we're paying attention to His quiet call.

The prophet Elijah learned this. You may know his story from reading 1 Kings 19. Elijah had endured multiple challenges and threats to his life. King Ahab and Queen Jezebel (*not* a Yes Sister!) were chasing him down after Jezebel massacred many other prophets.

It had been a long haul, and Elijah had done his best. But he was spent. Emptied. Done. In the wilderness, he prayed to die: "It is enough! Now, LORD, take my life" (v. 4 NKJV).

In the stillness of a cave hideout (while staying, remaining, resting, and being), Elijah laid out his exhaustion and loneliness before God and experienced the Lord in a fresh way—a way he may not have fully appreciated apart from this tough situation.

> Then [God] said, "Go out, and stand on the mountain before the LORD." And behold, the LORD passed by, and a great and strong wind tore into the mountains and broke the rocks in pieces before the LORD, but the LORD was not in the wind; and after the wind an earthquake, but the LORD was not in the earthquake; and after the earthquake a fire, but the LORD was not in the fire; and after the fire a still small voice. (1 Kings 19:11–12 NKJV)

When we practice staying, remaining, resting, and being in the shelter of the Lord's heart, we find security and endurance. We overcome.

This world urges us to take a different route—to trust that we are our own source of empowerment, that it's all up to us. A wise Yes Sister reminds us that isn't so. Sure, we want to be capable. But we also need to be realistically humble enough to see that storms most definitely can waste us and we weren't meant to handle them alone.

Author Dallas Willard, who is known for embracing the gifts (or "spiritual disciplines") of silence and solitude, writes, "When [Satan] undertook to draw Eve away from God, he did not hit her with a stick, but with an idea. It was with an idea that God could not be trusted and that she must act on her own to secure her own well-being."[1]

That, as Eve soon discovered, is dangerous thinking.

The unchanging God fights for us. He will deepen our dreams no matter what storm we're facing. He is not finished with our stories.

And as He did with Elijah, He will use other people to help us regain our footing.

Giving by Receiving

It's nice not to need. But it isn't realistic. It isn't even God's plan for us. He wants us to become familiar with being needy, because that's how we're drawn to Him and how we experience true overcoming power. It's also often how He connects us as one another's support system.

We miss out on our own character growth if we don't learn to receive well. More crucially, we miss the opportunity to lean into God to be filled and refilled.

Elijah received God's provision by way of His messenger. We need God's helpers too. Sometimes they come in the form of Yes Sisters.

You likely know someone who doesn't take a compliment or a hand up very well. Or perhaps you've been disappointed by someone's refusal of your offer to help.

We aren't talking about the perpetual "taker" who doesn't assume mature responsibility for her life, but the woman who feels like a burden unless she manages every detail solo.

That's not a health-giving model.

Receiving well is an art worth nurturing. We can actually *give back* by receiving well.

Let's acknowledge that part of ourselves that has a tough time holding out our hands—or heart—to accept another's offer. Receiving with grace and dignity establishes a down-to-earth, genuine, yet dignified model to follow. And it sends the message to the giver that it's okay if someday the situation is reversed. She is welcome to come to us when she has a need.

Receiving well invites reciprocated openness between Yes Sisters. It welcomes other women to loosen their own imaginary grip on their perceived capabilities, just as we released ours—without losing face.

Receiving well also improves teamwork and builds community. Leading by receiving is an uncommon way to bond us with the Yes Sister who has given to us. It lifts us both a little higher. When our face and voice reflect confident gratitude, we convey maturity not everyone understands, much less practices. It shows we are beautifully layered women of grace who are capable of holding our heads high no matter the challenges in front of us or the depth of our need.

Watch your Yes Sister's eyes brighten when you allow her the chance to feel necessary and of value to you. Intentionally give back to a giver by letting her know the difference she's made in your life. Your journey will be a richer experience with her as a part of it, and she'll be blessed in the process.

When I was at my neediest as an adult, flattened by depression and no income, my mother opened her home to me. For several months, I slept in her recliner. Night after night, she gave me the gift of sanctuary, safety, and security, and the freedom to be low for however long I needed.

I was able to—you might have guessed—stay, remain, rest, and be. It wasn't easy to be in that position of extended receiving. But we all get a turn at being paused somewhere along life's road.

It is not a bad thing to be paused. A pause in life, a slowdown, gives us the opportunity to face our need. God can build us stronger in our core during those times of receiving.

Those times also show us who our Yes Sisters are.

Quiet Availability

We might need a Yes Sister to take the reins for us when we're depleted of resources. Or we may simply need to know a Yes Sister is nearby while we figure things out for ourselves. Our best gift is to communicate with her so she understands where we're coming from when we say, "Thank you for your offer to help, but I'm not ready for it just yet."

When it's our turn to help, we are wise to pay attention to the other person's underlying vibes that hint when to step in assertively and when to hold back.

This dance of giving and waiting in the wings takes practice, thoughtfulness, and an unhurried style. Our quiet availability carries great influence.

Londa learned this lesson when she was in dire straits, and it equipped her to better help others in the future. Londa had always thrived on helping. Even as a young girl she loved riding her bike to a nearby retirement home to bring cookies to the residents. In high school, her class voted her "best volunteer." And in college, she headed up a peer-tutor program in her dorm. She prided herself on paying attention to what was going on in other people's lives.

However, it wasn't until Londa was in her early thirties, drowning in her triplets' spit-up and diaper pile, that she learned how to *accept* help. And she discovered the wonderful gift of quiet availability.

When she was pregnant, the women in her neighborhood had thrown her a baby shower and offered to be available to help her as she settled into motherhood with three newborns. Londa had thanked them but inwardly determined not to bother them. She'd figure it out.

Three months of maternity leave had seemed like plenty of time to get her household in smooth running order. In her job, she handled high-stress financial deals every day and navigated the concerns of dozens of coworkers. Three adorable little children ought to be manageable if she implemented her systems.

But late one morning, two months after bringing the babies home from the hospital, her son and both her tiny daughters screamed for three hours—after having awakened her every hour the previous night.

None of them had fevers or other signs of sickness. They'd been fed. She'd done everything the books instructed to soothe gassy tummies. All three had dry diapers. And none of them seemed inclined to fall asleep from exhaustion, even though their mother longed to do so.

Her husband was on a business trip, and she was short one arm to hold all the babies at once, as they demanded. Londa couldn't bear the thought of managing another long night on her own. Utterly spent and unraveling, she knew it was time to call for help before she made a dangerous blunder or collapsed.

Across the street, Candy answered Londa's call on the first ring and was out the door before Londa completed her first teary sentence. In the span of an hour, Candy calmed the babies and set up a plan with five other women in the neighborhood. All six of Londa's newest Yes Sisters enthusiastically promised to take turns calling Londa once a day, stopping by to rock an infant, change a diaper, give a bath, put supper in the oven, mop the floor, or give Londa time to take a shower.

"We've been waiting for you to give us the go-ahead," Candy said with a reassuring grin. "We've all been there! Most of us had only one baby screaming for our attention, much less three."

As Candy ushered Londa down the hall to nap for the rest of the afternoon, Londa marveled at the wisdom of women who knew how and when to respond to her needs. They'd known better than she had how challenging a baby could be and could imagine the exponentially more difficult task of managing three. But they hadn't forced their help.

Those neighborhood women unobtrusively modeled the art of being quietly available until Londa finally accepted their offer to come alongside her. Each of the women had called Londa during the first month after the babies were home to repeat their offers to help. But all of them had known not to push too hard. They'd sensed that, because of her personality and drive, Londa needed to reach the end of herself before she'd be ready to seek assistance.

After that experience, instead of jumping into every situation determined to fix things for someone else, Londa offered her availability to them and then prayed and remained watchful and ready to help when the time was right.

We share kinship in giving and receiving, no matter which role we're occupying.

In each example of struggle at the beginning of this chapter, Yes Sisters came alongside their fellow sisters in specific ways to help them endure. No one was abandoned—not by God or by the Yes Sisters He sent as His messengers.

We can't always fix every problem or silence every storm. But we can speak truth, encourage faith, and help in practical ways while reminding each other that we aren't finished with our journeys, and God will never be finished being our God.

A WORD FROM
a Yes Sister

Dr. Nicole LaBeach, *success strategist, relationship expert, author, and CEO of Volition Enterprises, Inc.*

A *Greater Love for* The Color Purple

I still remember the phone call.

The night passed unassuming until 1:00 a.m., when my brother called from California. He was distraught and in need of prayer about a family dynamic that was taking its toll. But when I interceded for him, something felt off.

I prayed but felt more and more unsettled. I couldn't ignore it. So after ending our conversation, I began to pray differently. For myself.

"Lord, show me what this is. I don't understand what's happening."

Within minutes, a text pinged on my husband's phone and catapulted my life into an unexpected tumble. One minute all was seemingly well and the next it was like the movie *The Matrix,* and I had just swallowed the blue pill of knowledge and understanding.

Before that moment, I had been part of what I thought was a loving, respectful, and admirable marriage. The next I was uncovering a cesspool of lies, deceptions, and manipulation that sought to unravel my world and incinerate my heart. It was as if a swarm of locusts had arrived and were quickly devouring everything I thought was real.

The next hours seemed the longest. What to do? What to say? How to feel? What to feel?

When everything first broke, I immediately went to the home of my best friend, Kimberlee. She did what I suppose any best friend would do. She listened, sympathized, and empathized. She cared for me as I felt the flood of information would surely drown me.

I was overcome with grief. Feeling lost and alone, I went home and curled up on my bed in the fetal position. Not only did my tears seem never-ending, but my thoughts also played mental acrobatics like I had never experienced. My heart felt like it was literally on fire.

The next day the doorbell rang. I couldn't move, so my husband answered it. A minute later, I heard a light tap on my bedroom door.

"Pudd?" Kimberlee used the nickname she had called me for almost twenty years. Through my swollen eyes and a flood of tears, she appeared as fuzzy as life felt. But I didn't need to see her clearly because she could see me. I didn't need to shift, move, or speak. Without hesitation, she got in the bed with me and began singing worship songs in my ear. Occasionally she stroked my hair and wiped my tears. As her tears met mine, her songs lobbied with the Lord. She carried a portion of my pain, anguish, and sorrow so I wouldn't have to do it alone.

Then she looked at me as only a best friend and sister-woman could and said, "You can do this, Pudd. We're gonna make it through this."

I was broken and in a heap of tiny little pieces, but she saw me whole again. She could see what I couldn't. She saw beyond my crisis and through the valley of the shadow of death. Not only could she see it, but she volunteered to take the journey with me. She said yes to helping heal my obliterated emotions. Her yes held a space for me to return to my whole self.

In that moment, she was a friend like the ones in *The Color Purple*. She was Ms. Celie to my Shug because "she scratched it out of my head when I was sick!"[1]

For her yes, I say, "Thank you!" For my peace now, I say, "Hallelujah!"

Chapter 11

We DO Get Second Chances—and Thirds . . .

> Return to me, for I have redeemed you.
>
> Isaiah 44:22 ESV

If you've read the book or seen the delightful miniseries *Anne of Green Gables*, you may remember this quote from Anne (that's Anne with an *e*, she'd pertly state): "Kindred spirits are not so scarce as I used to think. It's splendid to find out there are so many of them in the world."[1] Anne is famous for her flowery, over-the-top sayings, and she's always on the lookout for kindred spirits and bosom friends.

In addition to being smart and whimsical, Anne Shirley is a girl in dire need of a second chance—and a few Yes Sisters along the way. Anne may be fictional, but that doesn't stop her from being relatable. Her heart longs to belong, to revel in the freedom and inspiration to become all she was created to be.

But the story begins with Anne stuck in a spot.

After her parents die when she is a very young child, Anne is shuffled from house to house, wherever the needs are greatest. She goes not as a daughter, but as extra help no one has to pay. An undetermined time at each place further denies her the stability to feel settled anywhere.

For her first eleven years, Anne receives message after message that she will never have a chance to soar beyond the tragedy of her early life. She is a girl with treasured, unique hopes, who just needs a miracle or two to rescue her wounded spirit.

Anne's second chance finally comes when Matthew and Marilla Cuthbert send for an orphan to help on their farm.

With her heart open wide, ready to burst for the joy of it all, Anne travels to the Cuthberts' beautiful home, Green Gables.

Awe overtakes her on the carriage ride as she gazes at the beauty of this new environment. Flowering trees gather on both sides of the lane and wave their leaves in gentle celebration. Soon the vista opens up to greening hills that roll for miles.

And there, nestled up ahead, sits a cozy white farmhouse with gables and shutters painted green. Home. *Her* home. It is a place of Anne's dreams, a place to finally, finally belong. Hope and potential bubble up in her as a lifetime of heartache slips into the past.

Anne of Green Gables is a timeless classic, in part because a long-awaited good turn in a story is such a pleasure. We love the breath of fresh air a yes brings, a second chance at last.

One of my most significant second chances arrived between November 2015 and November 2016. I had no idea of the blessings that year would usher in.

In the autumn of 2015, I received a ticket for a cruise, during which I was to be honored as a media entrepreneur.

I was in the process of resigning from a short stint at Ball State University and had another job lined up. I didn't want the new position, but a lack of steady income didn't sound good to me. The magazine was growing, but the thought of not relying on a day job to pay the bills brought anxiety.

So I packed up my desk and said goodbye to my coworkers. Excitement about the cruise mingled with apprehension about starting another office job when I returned—another job that would never fill my heart.

My discontent was the God-given kind. He was nudging me out of an unfulfilling safety net in order to lead me into His next new for me.

One nudge came through the boss I was leaving behind. Before I walked away from that Ball State position for good, he held up a copy of *HOPE* and regarded me pointedly. "You do not need to waste your time working in that other job," he said.

My heart may have skipped a beat or two. His words stayed with me throughout the entire vacation. I had much to consider as the big ship carried me over the ocean waves.

That trip brought a measure of clarity and reaffirmed my hope for a future free from unhealthy limitations. But I still had questions: I wanted to focus full-time on the magazine, but could it provide for my family's needs? Was I capable of making an all-in run at it? Was the idea foolish . . . or foolish only if God wasn't leading me in that direction?

Just what was He telling me to do?

I prayed long and hard for discernment to hear Him clearly. I did not want to get this wrong. My kids and I had been through plenty, and we needed stability.

We needed hope. Little did I know at that point how God would repeatedly confirm that we also needed *HOPE*.

Fresh peace and faith were gaining life and footing in me.

But when I got back home, I second-guessed myself and played it safe once more. I began that new job. I allowed my nerves to interrupt my faith a while longer.

Three months inched by while I put in my time. Eight hours a day, five days a week, the questions and prayers continued to roll in my thoughts. And an underlying anticipation never stopped growing.

I was newly single, and my youngest son, Jordan, and I were staying with my mother. My two older kids were away at college. Those ninety days allowed me time to catch my breath and gain confidence.

But it was time for me to figure out my next steps. I knew I had crazy faith to believe I'd been giving hope to women all those years. As I fell asleep each night on my mother's recliner with her dog, Argo, curled up next to me, I began to trust fully that God was offering the same hope to me.

Eventually, the Lord calls all of us to put our money where our mouth is. This was my time.

My Yes Sisters were there to inspire me to step out in faith. They told me the magazine was making a difference. "It is really something, Angie."

And my mother never stopped encouraging me either. "You were made for this," she said.

Decision time came in late February 2016 after a traffic accident—someone plowed into the back of my mom's car while I was driving. While I was off work recovering, I decided to submit my resignation. I'd worked too hard to build the magazine not to give it a chance to become all it could be. I knew it was time to dive in with boundless faith in God and a growing belief in myself.

I needed Yes Sisters to help me see and think clearly during those daunting days. Maurita told me to get a desk first. "Fix up your corner," she instructed. Somehow Maurita had the wisdom to know that organizing an actual office area would make the transition to being a full-time magazine publisher official to me.

With her help, I found a nineteen-dollar desk and set up my laptop on it next to a recliner. A TV tray for my printer completed my office space. It was humble and it was mine. I loved it. Every day when I woke up, I went to work—and my commute took all of three steps!

Those were cozy, challenging months that I spent tucked in a safe place with my mother and son. Her house was a home full of peace as I moved into this new realm of my work life. I was a full-time publisher.

Over the next year, God brought several more second chances my way. I've come to believe that starting over is a good thing—a second chance is a refresh. It's a reminder of God's grace and goodness. If we fall, He's there to lift us back up and help us begin again. Second chances solidify our faith during those tough times.

In 2016, I found so much satisfaction and contentment resting in God's arms. I knew He had me and I was okay. Having Yes Sisters was an added bonus, another way He smiled on me to let me know He always wants what is best for me, even when the path takes me through difficulties. Difficulties are ways for God to show us more of Himself.

God's faithfulness that year became an anchor I continue to refer to when I need a reminder that He will never cease to be in my life. The growth I experienced that year steadied me later on when the magazine faced losses and setbacks.

Redemption Promise

Back at Green Gables, Anne barely moves past the threshold before her second chance is snatched from her. Stern and practical Marilla chastises Matthew for bringing home a *girl* when they'd asked for a *boy*. What use do they have for a girl?

Anne steps in to claim her second chance, only for life to shove her right back out the door.

Her hopes are crushed. "I might have known this was all too beautiful to last."

"Well, well, there's no need to cry so about it." Marilla's cool response isn't exactly the motherly comfort Anne needs.

"Oh, this is the most *tragical* thing that ever happened to me."[2]

After all she's been through, this rejection tastes the bitterest of all because she thought she had finally had the blessings of home and family. Being cast off is entirely too familiar to her. Would the nos ever run out?

Anne Shirley could top the list of souls in need of another chance. And a Yes Sister. Marilla, too, for that matter.

It turns out that Anne does get a third chance when the Cuthberts let her stay at Green Gables. At last she has found her heart's desire.

As she grows through her teen years, she not only softens Marilla's stoic emotions but also finds several Yes Sisters ("bosom friends" and "kindred spirits," in her words) who champion her and nourish her starving soul. She does the same for them.

It's a heartwarming story with a simple underlying reminder that even if circumstances make us feel like we're at the end and out of options, all hope is never lost.

Second and third chances are not fictional concepts. The redos are heaven-sent, God's own idea. He knows how desperately we need redemption—from the wounds of our circumstances and other people's choices, as well as from our own sins.

God isn't surprised that we are still prone to sinning and making mistakes. And none of the disappointments that threaten our well-being escape His sovereign care.

Viewing our lives as repeated opportunities for redos offers us a refreshing approach to this journey on earth. It's humbling and freeing all at once, mellowing any delusion that we won't need grace again and again, daily.

God established the concept of *redemption,* which has to be on the short list of the most wondrous, life-giving words ever. He loves to redeem what is lost. God doesn't see our mistakes as failures. Our mistakes and our ongoing recovery from them mean we are growing. *Grace changes us.*

In Joel 2:25, we read a promise God made to the Israelites regarding their threadbare hope. He said He would "restore to [them] the years that the swarming locust has eaten" (ESV).

He has the same heart toward you and me. And He's building His heart into ours so we're strong to build up our Yes Sisters.

Second-Chance Sisters

Yes Sisters help us find our second chances, rebuild, renew, restart, or transform. Yes Sisters will say, "You can have a great life! Let's walk together." If you don't have someone telling you this right now, I am here to be your Yes Sister and share what I've learned to be true: you can start over again.

When we recognize the transformative power of grace and forgiveness in our own lives, we are empowered to fearlessly offer others another chance as well. God has allowed me to help others build their brand and get their start. He has even given me this theme of Yes Sisterhood for a purpose beyond my own fulfillment.

Redemption is the power behind the second chance, and God invites you and me to take part in it. When we're on the lookout for evidence of His work in our lives, opportunities abound for Him to provide for others through us.

November 2015 to November 2016 was a year loaded with redemption's richness. From God's view, each year is just as full.

Standing next to my Yes Sister Cheryl in the autumn of 2016, with my toes dipped into the warm sand and the ever-tumbling surf in sight, I understood a little more what redemption and second chances look like in reality—they were no longer just the stuff of dreams.

A WORD FROM
a Yes Sister

Tricia Goyer, bestselling author and speaker

A Legacy of Yes

When I was pregnant with my son Cory, I was seventeen and so ashamed. I'd been a cheerleader, and my boyfriend was on the football team. I chose to have my baby. So there I was in school with people talking about me behind my back. My boyfriend got a new girlfriend right away. I was so embarrassed that I finished the work I needed to graduate high school at home.

It was the darkest time of my life. I'd sleep all day, then watch recorded soap operas at night. Because I was an honor student, I didn't have many credits to complete. I'd do my homework in two hours and the rest of the week I focused on being depressed while my friends were going on with their senior year. Keep in mind, this was before cell phones and text messaging. My friends were still doing their thing, and I was alone.

Then my mom and grandma's Bible study group, which included the pastor's wife and some other ladies, asked me to join them. I did *not* want to go. But they invited me to lunch, which was at my grandma's house, so I started going to the Bible study. However, I would literally fall asleep in my grandma's La-Z-Boy, so I wasn't even paying attention.

Then the pastor's wife asked to come over and pray with me. I literally turned my back on her and laid in bed, depressed. But she sat in the room with me. I knew she was praying, even though I wasn't giving her the courtesy of my attention. Eventually, she stood up, put her hand on my arm, and simply said, "I love you. God loves you." Then she left.

Those words started chipping away at the hard wall around my heart. When the women from the Bible study threw me a baby shower, I realized that maybe if those women still loved me, then God loved me too. If they could reach out and want to spend time with me, if they could encourage me and celebrate my baby, then maybe God loved me.

It was because of them that I said, "Okay, God, I've messed up. But if you can do anything with my life, please do." The love those women showed me opened my heart to Christ.

That's why I lead teen moms now, why I conduct a teen moms support group. I want to do for other young women what those women did for me. These teens get the looks. They get people talking about them at the grocery store. I want to be the one who says, "You're going to be a good mom. Your kid's going to be amazing." I want to be that encouragement like those women were to me. I'm passing on a legacy of what they gave me. Once I gave my life to God, I went totally for Him.

The pastor's wife, the woman I turned my back on and didn't want to look at, is now my mother-in-law. Her son asked me out soon after I gave birth to Cory.

When John and I started dating, she was excited for us because she had seen the difference in my life. That just shows you grace right there. Her twenty-two-year-old son was dating this seventeen-year-old young lady who had just had a baby. And she was okay with it because she could see God's hand in it all.

My mother-in-law, Darlyne, believed in me and loved me, and the other ladies at the church loved me. Because of them, I'm now doing the same with the teen moms around me.

Chapter 12

We ARE Finding Our Way

> I will instruct you and teach you in the way you should go;
> I will counsel you with my eye upon you.
>
> Psalm 32:8 ESV

There I was in church, surrounded by misguided people and listening to the condemnation in the sermons. Nearly everyone around me was constrained, unhappy, and bound by false doctrine, arrogance, and fear. I'd become chained to a miserable place.

I couldn't remain there any longer. I was lost and yearned for freedom, but I didn't know what to do. I assumed—partly because of my history of abuse—that the problem lay within me. I must not be "doing church" right. I must not understand what God's Word really says. The lies that had been spread about me for years must have been true.

No. No, they weren't. So now what?

My past affected how I saw myself. And how I understood God. I needed to find out what healing looked like.

In 2016, after making several major changes in my work, home, and church life, I began the journey of truly finding my way. I felt like I was getting to know God, as well as myself, more deeply. I became acquainted with the real me, freed from being relegated to the sidelines of life.

I hadn't really understood who I was before that year. I hadn't been allowed to make my opinion known or consider my own needs, much less express them. I'd been programmed to believe that joy and enjoyment were off-limits. I never thought I'd be allowed to travel or own better than a worn-out version of anything. Most of all, I didn't see God clearly, or my true identity in relation to Him.

Those toxic beliefs melted away throughout 2016. New vitality budded and bloomed in their place. I began planning to one day buy my own comfortable bed that offered good sleep, as well as a stove with working burners and a new refrigerator to hold an abundance of food.

When the beach awakened me late that year to my love for beautiful surroundings, I marveled at the wonders of God's creation with clearer vision: the flutter of the leaves, the roll of the surf, the blueness of the sky. It all looked miraculous to me. I began inviting celebration and fun into my every day.

At last I felt found. Second chances are wonderful, and we need them like we need air to breathe.

Yet, in all the freshness, challenges still lay ahead of me. New beginnings can require us to roll up our sleeves and get to work finding our way. The Lord might give us a nugget of something new, but He wants to see our faith in action in response.

At times, we may still doubt we'll ever move beyond a hardship. We keep our heads down and work diligently, but it still may seem as if we're hardly moving. Finding our way can feel more like we're lost than we are moving forward.

The years since 2016 most definitely have brought highs and lows. Cloudy circumstances sprinkled themselves among the blessings and made me question whether I had correctly interpreted God's direction for me. What would I have done without encouraging women around me to help me recalibrate when I drifted off track emotionally?

Together with my Yes Sisters, I started to understand that following a new way would involve healthy change, grace for the trial and error I would experience, and relentless hope.

● ● ●

Healthy Change

The changes I made in my church life helped me break free of some unhealthy relationships. I see clearly now that the control I'd been under was not from God. It was human-based, power-based. Switching my church home was hard, but I don't regret it. In the years since, I've found what true Christianity is meant to be and what it means to be part of a healthy, growing church community.

We often fear change and stay put in what's familiar—the so-so that isn't necessarily what's best for us. We can become trapped in a variety of unhealthy situations. It might involve a relationship, a job, an organization, a friendship, or a church. God's yes could ask us to make courageous shifts, maybe even leave the status quo to move forward and find His new way for us.

Putting space between ourselves and negative environments or strained relationships can improve those situations to the point that it's possible for us to reengage with much healthier dynamics in place. At times, distance can bring long-needed clarity to conflicting perceptions.

All relationships go through seasons of highs and lows, including those between Yes Sisters.

Nadia and Francesca are lifelong Yes Sisters who saw each other through teenage drama and college life. Then they shared an apartment for a few years as single twentysomethings. Their friendship carried the blessing of knowing many of the experiences, wounds, and successes that had formed each other early on.

But, eventually, too much of a good thing created tension in their close quarters and kept both women from growing individually. Over several months, animosity snowballed to a breaking point. Resentment and anger tainted every conversation, until an icy atmosphere chilled any communication at all. It was time to move on.

Life took them in different directions. Years passed when Nadia and Francesca didn't talk to each other at all. Each woman benefited from space and time to provide perspective on how they had contributed to the problems in their friendship. Maturity nudged both of them to reach out with apologies.

Ten years after the final big argument that sent them in separate ways, Nadia and Francesca spoke on the phone. Through humility and honesty, they renewed their friendship. Both are better for the ups and downs that have marked their journey as Yes Sisters.

Healthy distance can be the straightest path to future restoration. Even bonds as strong as those between Yes Sisters can stretch and fray throughout a lifetime of being human.

Distance can also be the first step when circumstances call for a permanent break. Endings are hard, even when it's obvious they're needed. If we have become dependent on false comfort that stunts our growth, we may not recognize how enmeshed we are in a bad situation. The pain of remaining might seem less traumatic than moving in a different direction. But in the long run, this isn't true.

Creating healthy space deserves immense sensitivity and care, discernment from the Lord, godly counsel, biblical wisdom, and healthy caution.

The change may be an inner one, requiring us to leave behind a toxic perspective, habit, or focus. Or the shift may be outwardly visible, involving situational and lifestyle rearrangements.

Recovering my life and my ability to thrive in God's love involved both types. The moves were overwhelming and scary—and they were transforming. I am *here*, continuing to find my way, because I left *there*. Here is where I belong, right in the middle of God's yes for me.

Grace for Trial and Error

My first two conferences were complete flops. The sponsorship money we needed didn't come through. While processing what went wrong, I learned not everyone on my team was committed to pulling together a good conference. This became a weeding-out season so I could find stronger helpers who shared my vision.

When I lost those two entire magazine issues due to a distributor's bankruptcy, old doubts and fears again threatened to level me. Lies from the past returned with their wicked whispers that I should give up and resign myself to failure—it had been a nice run, but maybe it was never meant to be long-lasting.

My trial-and-error experiences were not enjoyable. They triggered fear and doubt and caused me to second-guess myself. But they also taught me invaluable lessons about pushing through tough times without losing focus of my greater purpose. They showed me the value of surrounding myself with key people who have my back and are willing to point me in better directions.

Seasons of foggy foresight are completely normal. When we tackle something new but can't see every detail of what's ahead, we will have days when it feels like we're barely keeping our heads above water. Thankfully, trial and error grows our wisdom, helping us proactively ground ourselves and make vital course corrections.

Margins

If you're like me, when you step out in faith for a yes you believe God wants you to pursue, you might feel you have to put 100 percent of your heart into it. While this is true, it's also true that you need margins for rest, laughter, and loving the people around you.

I had to adjust my schedule when it became clear that my kids were getting my leftovers instead of my primary energy, which I'd been pouring into my work. The imbalance had worn us all down.

What did I learn? We can't fill up the entire page of our days and hours. We must leave space for peace and joy and beauty. Create pockets of time to go for walks without our phones, turn up some music and dance in the living room, take our kids out for ice cream or to the park, or cuddle up with a good book.

Sometimes the most important margin is just to be quiet. Quiet margin fills us up creatively and reconnects us with God.

Yes Sister Time

Spending time with our Yes Sisters is part of creating margins too, but prioritizing time with them needs to be intentional. Reach out to your Yes Sisters instead of continuing to plow along alone. Schedule regular "meetings" with them one-on-one or in groups to rejuvenate and get filled back up.

Phone calls, texts, and emails serve a purpose. But none of those build relationship like in-person time does. You'll move forward faster by slowing down and getting pumped up by your sisters—and by motivating them as well.

Connect the Dots

Sit down with a journal to record and reflect on important milestones. Try to see the big picture. A significant opportunity doesn't just happen. That opportunity exists because God brought together many details.

Can you see how God used mistakes, failures, and triumphs to open doors? Write down whatever comes to mind. When we connect the dots God has laid out for us, we see the journey instead of feeling lost in a string of seemingly unrelated incidents.

Also connect the dots of your Yes Sister relationships. It always amazes me to see how one friendship leads to other friendships to still others. We wear this string of friendship pearls close to our hearts.

Relentless Hope

Did a Bible verse speak to you this morning? Did you hear a quote that encouraged you? Did you pick a theme word as a sort of motto for the year? Write down any bit of encouragement on a Post-it Note and put it around your home and office. When you're feeling discouraged, the reminders will help you see beyond the frustration or fear.

You can even ask your Yes Sisters to create reminders for you. What a joy it is to hear what our Yes Sisters are speaking into us.

If it weren't for a few Yes Sisters who helped me get back on track, I doubt the magazine or this book would exist today. Failed conferences, financial setbacks, naysayers—all of those challenges frayed my hope. Cheryl and Liz, in particular, kept the faith when I misplaced it. They met with me for a strategy session and showed me that I was focusing too much on the negative.

They pointed out correctly that I couldn't see the value of what I had created from nothing. "You're like our hero," they said.

Hadn't *I* been mentored by *them*?

"And the fact that you're still here and still publishing in some way shows God's hand in this," they said. "He has something more for you because you're still here."

I had never looked at it that way.

They told me the magazine was just the vehicle to get me somewhere I never anticipated going. It was truly God's baby more than my own. I was confused, but was He? Never. He would see to its growth, and mine too.

Those sisters modeled for me the critical importance of choosing to have a productive perception, of choosing to defend God's truth and power in my life when all seems lost.

There's a key truth that impacts everything: *Will you choose to defend who God says He is and the victory He claims for you?*

Regardless of how things look from an earthly vantage, will you trust Him to hold you and keep you going, as He promises? Or will you cave to shortsighted discouragement? These are big questions to ask whether things are going peachy or not so swimmingly.

The most daunting faith steps when I followed God led to my greatest areas of healing and blessing. The loss of those two magazine issues led to a new opportunity for the publication that I might not have tried otherwise—the internet. We focused on our online version, which I can see in hindsight was perfect timing.

Sometimes the worst thing can turn into the best thing.

We can't give up when we feel lost. And often, we aren't as lost as we think. We may wind our way through darkness that is about to open into more light than we ever imagined. And our Yes Sisters can help clear our vision. We *will* find our way, and it'll be better than expected.

I am making a way in the wilderness and streams in the wasteland.

Isaiah 43:19

A WORD FROM
a Yes Sister

Tamela Mann, Grammy Award winner
and NAACP Award winner

The Friendship Anchor

How do you find inspiration? A movie that inspires me to keep loving and living is *Beaches*. Starring Bette Midler and Barbara Hershey, this 1988 American comedy-drama is all about the power of friendship.

I've always loved this movie, and eventually, I got my husband, David, to like it too. The story shares many jewels to having successful friendships, in life and in love. Through thick and thin, in highs and lows, we need the anchor of friendships. Our friendships with other women can even carry over to the friendship we share with our spouse.

Temporary things will change. But if you have friendship, you have the key to longevity, life, and love!

Chapter 13

We HAVE Shoulders to Cry On or to Stand On

Two are better than one,
　　because they have a good return for their labor:
If either of them falls down,
　　one can help the other up.

Ecclesiastes 4:9–10

I was click-clacking my thoughts onto my keyboard one day when an incoming email popped up on my screen.

It was from my friend Cheryl. She and I had connected when she was also a magazine publisher, years before our trip to the beach. Cheryl's been a great Yes Sister who's always ready to offer a boost of confidence or a nudge in the right direction.

She was the one who saw my biggest struggles and wisely told me to figure out where they started. What was their origin? She never judged and always believed in me. She pushed me to keep going in spite of obstacles and past nos. It was because of her that I began to believe God does have beautiful things prepared for me.

"When the time is right, you'll be able to enjoy them," she said.

Cheryl helped me set goals and strategies for my growing business. When details overwhelmed me, she somehow knew I needed more than a "You go, girl." With just the right tone, she spoke direction into my confusion and wasn't shy about doing it. And I wasn't shy about accepting her counsel.

She even organized an out-of-state strategy session with two other Yes Sisters, Vetta and Liz. We spent a weekend planning what the next year of HOPE would look like.

I don't know where I'd be without Cheryl's help.

But that day I could sense from her email that something was going on with her.

"I'm just having a moment," she explained. Her business wasn't progressing the way she had envisioned, and she couldn't shake her discouragement. It seemed to her that everyone else was moving forward while she felt stuck in neutral.

I knew that nagging feeling. Because of the way she and others had lifted me up, I knew she needed a shift in perspective and a nudge of encouragement to make a few key changes.

"You're like me," I told her. "You want to do it all, but you need reinforcements."

I was able to help her start an intern program and develop her media kit so she could pursue speaking opportunities. Together we adjusted her goals so they became more accessible.

I've certainly needed a great deal of practical help over the years, and my sisters have too. Cheryl and another friend, Keisha, and other Yes Sisters have told me they've had to ask for assistance at low points. Allowing ourselves to be vulnerable and real with one another creates richness and depth, understanding and acceptance in our relationships. And we experience being loved for who we truly are, warts and all.

Being willing and bold enough to make my needs known became

a turning point in my life. It also reinforced to me what treasures we become for one another as shoulders of support.

● ● ●

Learning to Lean

None of us can do it all, not only from time to time but *ever*. And that's a beautiful thing. When we admit our lack to one another, we invite growth and closeness. We feel the security of being cared for, and we learn from one another in ways we never expected.

After we fuss and fume over a problem about which we have no or little expertise, we can seek out a person experienced in that issue. Turning to an expert or calling out for help isn't a sign of weakness; it's a sign of wisdom.

And *need* is not a synonym for *weakness*. Even if what we're lacking does reveal a weak spot, it is merely a launching point for further character development as we learn to lean into others for help.

We discover new approaches and fresh angles in problem-solving. We also see that admitting we don't always have the resources on our own is not necessarily a death blow to our pride.

When I am tempted to weather the stormy seas of life alone, God reminds me He has brought me Yes Sisters to hold on to and steady me in the raging wind. God is my anchor, but my Yes Sisters are life preservers.

They've taught me a great deal about loosening my grip on my fear and shame and accepting their support. Those are not easy lessons. Moving past whatever makes us want to hide our true selves from others can be hard won.

As we grow up, we expend significant emotional energy finetuning how we adapt to our environment and to real or perceived feedback from others. We self-protect by withholding parts of ourselves in order to function as tidily as possible—to feel as acceptable as possible. But each of us has an authentic self that longs to be fully known and accepted through and through.

In *Self to Lose—Self to Find*, Marilyn Vancil writes of the difference between our adapted selves and our authentic selves. (I love it when I discover Yes Sisters in books!)

She writes, "Our Authentic Self was created to reflect God's image in a way only we can do . . . We will find our greatest fulfillment in becoming who God created us to become."[1]

Our adapted self, however, is similar to what the Bible calls our old self. "Put off your old self, which belongs to your former manner of life . . . be renewed in the spirit of your minds, and . . . put on the new self, created after the likeness of God" (Eph. 4:22–24 ESV).

Each of us carries unique baggage we've collected over the years. It's weighty and full of those parts of ourselves we don't feel safe revealing to other people. Those parts that bring feelings of fear, shame, condemnation, insecurity, lack of control, etc. We don't like to deal with them ourselves, so we most definitely don't want others to know about them.

Many of us have experienced friendships with other women that left us feeling betrayed. So we shy away from letting ourselves get close enough to lean on someone else for support when we need it, lest we end up hurt again. Friendship hurts can put us on guard about showing the true "us."

But because our authentic self is the one God created us to be, trying to pass off any other version never works.

We become our adapted selves because we got the notion that our real selves weren't quite enough, weren't altogether acceptable, or not fully lovable. So how do we find the safety to be authentic?

The answer lies in thoughtful vulnerability.

The Safety of Vulnerability

Nobody lives in a vacuum. Our progress is affected by other people. And we affect everyone we come in contact with every day. We always make an impact, whether our influence echoes across the globe or doesn't extend beyond our own front door.

Since our efforts don't always yield the positive effects we desire or receive the responses we think we need, is it any wonder we have mixed feelings about taking the risk to be vulnerable? We are wise to tread with caution when choosing whom to open up to (and when). Vulnerability only works with trusted women. Not everyone can or should earn Yes Sister status.

But we are safe with true Yes Sisters. Yes Sisters have earned our trust and the right to cradle those sacred parts of our history, the places in our souls God wants to heal and reveal His strength and love. They remain committed to pointing us toward the beauty God intends to unpack from each no in our collection of baggage.

A Yes Sister is a woman who, when you answer, "I'm fine," responds with, "Super. Now tell me how you're really doing."

She asks because she wants to know—for your good. She's a true supportive shoulder. She's not asking so she has dirt to wield against you at an opportune moment. Nor is she looking for ways to feel better about herself or thinking, *At least my life isn't as messy at present.*

Wise Vulnerability

In the past, I have struggled with being open and vulnerable and letting others help me. I was ashamed of my economic status and didn't want others to know what was going on behind the outward image I worked hard to present. No one at the unhealthy church I attended knew the authentic me. The real me wouldn't have been accepted by or acceptable to those people.

I hesitated to speak of my dream to bring hope to other women because I lacked confidence to take it seriously myself, and I couldn't bear any hint of ridicule. Even when I was enjoying some success with *HOPE*, I defaulted to my adapted self in order to feel as if I could belong among other professional women. Although I discovered numerous precious soul sisters I now count as Yes Sisters, I crossed paths with naysayers too.

It's tough when your insecurities are confirmed by other people.

Someone who can't seem to celebrate your successes or treat you as an equal colleague may be trying to cover her own insecurities. But she may only be fooling herself. Inauthenticity can't hide itself forever.

Yes Sisters don't mistake another's success as a reflection of their own value. They celebrate others without feeling threatened. My sisters have been the first to remind me of what really matters. And it isn't social status, economic advancement, or human accolades. Those can change in an instant.

Yes Sisters help you see your identity and build your life and live your purpose with Him as your foundation.

Tall Shoulders, Expansive Outlook

Sir Isaac Newton is known for saying, "If I have seen further, it is by standing upon the shoulders of giants."[2]

Whether our shoulders currently support others or we're the ones needing the lift, we all gain a more expansive understanding of God's broad love when we help one another look up. Shared comfort in the freedom to live as the unique women God created us to be helps us stand taller. At these heights, we're able to recognize the vastness of hope.

A WORD FROM
a Yes Sister

Vetta Cash, *educator, writer, minister, entrepreneur*

Leaning on One Another

The people (positive or negative) who get the highest percentage of my attention are by default my greatest influences. I continuously evaluate who these people are and why they hold such a prestigious position in my life. They influence the direction of my life more than my education, expertise, and experiences combined. Therefore, I owe it to myself, and my future, to identify and prioritize those personal influencers.

Angelia is a member of my circle of influence. Our friendship is genuine, transparent, and therapeutic. We created a safe environment for honest discussions about what is really going on in our lives. Our conversations are not about the ins and outs of *HOPE for Women* magazine. They are not about me planning for Breathe: The Annual Women's Emotional Health Conference. We don't talk about other women, family, etc. We have created a space to talk about us. I want to know how she is doing, and she asks the same about me. No competition or judgment, just two sister-friends fully invested in each other's well-being.

We are professional women who balance many responsibilities in ministry, business, and our families. We have honest conversations away from the "boss chair" with a person who sincerely cares.

Chapter 14

We CAN Handle the Truth

Guide me in your truth and teach me,
for you are God my Savior,
and my hope is in you all day long.

Psalm 25:5

"So sorry I'm late," Brielle said as she exhaled. She swung her bag over a chair and sat down across from Carmen. The restaurant buzzed with the activity of Monday afternoon patrons.

Carmen offered a small smile. She wasn't sure whether to wait for Brielle to bring up her family's upcoming move or dive right in and ask why her friend had withheld such an important detail. All morning Carmen had stewed inside, unable to shake the hurt. She wished she knew how to handle it. For now she would act as normal as possible.

The women looked over the menu and placed their orders, then caught each other up on their families and work, but Brielle said nothing about moving. The hands on the wall clock seemed to progress swiftly while they finished their soup and sandwiches.

"We missed you at Emerson's party," Carmen finally said when their coffee arrived. Brielle had RSVP'd that she and her husband

and their kids would be at Carmen's daughter's tenth birthday party, but they never showed up.

Brielle blinked, her coffee cup poised near her mouth. "Yes, her party . . . I'm sorry. I should have called to let you know we had a last-minute change of plans. Something important came up that we had to deal with."

Carmen nodded slowly and shrugged to press Bri for a better explanation. The two families never missed birthday events for each other's kids.

"I am sorry, Carmen. I should have called you. Can you trust me that it was important?"

Carmen slapped a sugar packet against her palm before tearing it open and shaking the crystals into her coffee. With any luck, maybe it would sweeten the bitter taste growing in her heart too.

A moment passed in awkward silence. Carmen glanced at Brielle and wasn't surprised to see her friend fidgeting with her purse, her phone, her coffee cup—anything, it seemed, to deflect the direction of the conversation. Why was it so hard to tell her about the move?

Finally, Carmen cleared her throat decisively. Ignoring the warning that she might be overstepping, she forged ahead. "I imagine if your change of plans had something to do with selling your house, then yes, that would be important."

Brielle's jaw dropped. She closed her mouth and swallowed slowly, her focus at last meeting Carmen's with honesty in her eyes. "How did you find out?" she asked quietly.

"Melanie." Releasing the truth only made Carmen's ire rise more. Both of their daughters were in Melanie Richmond's fourth-grade class. How could Brielle have told the girls' teacher but not her?

Brielle sighed heavily as her shoulders drooped.

"When were you planning to share your big news with me?" Carmen heard the hurt in her tone but didn't feel like hiding it from Brielle. She wanted Brielle to *answer* her, not just sit there.

But Brielle just stared at her.

"Why aren't you saying anything? Why would you suddenly move your kids across the country?" She shook her head. "When? When is this happening?"

"Carmen, stop."

The snap of Brielle's voice halted Carmen's vent. Brielle waved a hand toward Carmen. "*This* is why I didn't tell you. I was afraid you'd go off." She took a deep breath before continuing. "I don't need criticism now. I'm having a hard enough time without having to justify our reasons."

Carmen opened her mouth to say something, but Brielle held up a hand to hold her off. Carmen leaned back in the booth and waited, which felt odd.

"I was thinking of telling you today. I'd hoped you would be happy for us. Or at least understanding."

Awareness dawned uncomfortably in Carmen. Regret crept over her. How in the world could she have been so selfish? She should have been happy for them.

"You know Jared's job has been very stressful the past couple of years."

Carmen nodded.

Tears pooled in Brielle's eyes. "It's been awful, actually. He hasn't found anything different in the area, and it's only gotten worse for him. I've begged him for months to look outside the state. Anything would be better than staying where he is. Well, he finally got an offer—and yes, it's with a company a thousand miles away."

Carmen shook her head. "Why couldn't you tell me that?"

"Because I knew you'd react like you did. I knew it would upset you. I've hurt so much already for all the criticism my husband has taken at work. I couldn't take on yours too." She paused to wipe her tears with a paper napkin. "You know I'll miss you. But I need your support in this, Carmen."

I knew you'd react like you did. Ugh. In an instant, Carmen's self-righteous anger melted away. How could she have thought only of herself? No wonder Brielle didn't want to trust her with something so valuable. Carmen felt tears well in her own eyes and let them fall.

She reached across the table and gripped her friend's hand. "*I'm* really sorry, Bri. I bombed this one. And to think you knew I would." She shook her head, as if that could shift the truth. "I do want to hear all about what's going on. Please give me another chance?"

A shaky smile crept over Brielle's face. "I was hoping you'd say that. Thank you."

• • •

How the truth can sting! Have you ever felt "caught" in a misstep? It's so humbling. Our adapted selves don't want our shortcomings found out—it's the whole reason we've worked so hard to hide our authentic selves in the first place.

When my Yes Sisters told me my church environment was unhealthy, I was relieved. But I also felt uneasy because I hadn't gotten myself out of there sooner. When another sister pointed out that I wasn't valuing my work enough to ask for adequate compensation, I cringed a little, even though she meant the comment for my good. And when others advised me about tipping and valet parking and dressing to fit my professional role, I had to welcome the humble feeling as I welcomed their guidance. I didn't know as much as they did in those areas. But each time I've listened to truth in a safe setting, it has yielded growth.

My Yes Sisters have modeled for me how to share the truth well so that I felt validated even when I had to face my vulnerabilities and missteps. Over the years, I've had opportunities to be on the other side of truth-telling for the good of others I care about.

Each time a Yes Sister has told me I need to be more assertive about healthy boundaries or to stand up for myself or to expect more for my life or to forgive someone, their affirmations mixed with my entrenched doubts. Confirmation that our weaker areas are obvious to others doesn't feel good, even if the honesty comes from our most faithful Yes Sisters.

But we need the truth. Life doesn't work well without it. Keeping our hearts wide open for the truth about ourselves allows us to accept it and grow from it.

Difficult-to-hear honesty offered in a life-giving way is a treasure. Yes Sisters practice the art of truth-in-love with us. They bring Proverbs 25:11 to life because their words "fitly spoken [are] like apples of gold in a setting of silver" (ESV).

Gentle Truth, Secure Grace

Even though we don't want our failures and foibles found out, our adapted selves can't bring us real joy, contentment, or belonging. Adapted selves live in a world of illusion instead of reality. They miss the richness of true life. It's in our human shortcomings, mistakes, and missteps that we experience grace.

Grace's role isn't to transform what's perfect.

Grace comes to the broken. To you and me and everyone else on the planet who receives it. And what's even sweeter, God's grace melds beautifully with His truth. A difficult truth spoken with grace can build us up instead of tear us down.

God knows what character qualities each of us needs to grow, and He has never once received news about who we are. He never has reason to respond, "Wow, I hadn't realized that about her. I'm shocked!"

He knows us through and through, and He loves to love us securely, even as He matures us.

Yes Sisters who have received His grace are effective truth-tellers. They understand that genuine truth is never meant to diminish, but to beautify. That kind of honesty always, always, always benefits us, even when we initially feel its sting.

We *can* handle genuine truth because grace is the soft cushion we can fall back on. We can even learn to seek out truth, to value humility in ourselves as much as in other people.

Our weaknesses and mistakes do not make us failures. They make us human beings with great potential. They allow us to understand more about God's love for us.

It's even possible for our faults to unite us as Yes Sisters better than our strengths and accomplishments can. That's because our authentic selves breathe freely when we are truthfully and securely known.

Careful Sourcing of Truth

Today's culture would have us believe that *truth* is an ambiguous concept. My truth, your truth, his truth, her truth, etc. With all the versions of "truth" out there, how are we to trust feedback from others?

Just what is the truth about truth?

Can you believe Janie when she tells you that your input at a meeting was spot-on? More than once you've watched her compliment others' ideas in team meetings, only to tell you privately that those ideas were inadequate. Her "truth" seems to justify dishonesty when it suits her purposes. What else might she be deceptive about?

And when Shawna steers you away from buying a dress you love, saying it isn't worth the price, only to show up wearing it herself the next week? Her "truth" appears to be founded on competitiveness or selfishness. Can you trust her to wholeheartedly be a sister who cheers you on?

And Gracie is unwilling to offer constructive criticism, even when you ask her for it. Everything's always dandy in her world of bubbles and sunflowers. Her excuse is that we all need more positivity. That much is true. But unity cannot happen where there's no room for iron sharpening iron (Prov. 27:17).

At the heart of a Yes Sister's influence is her source of truth. Keeping God's Word as her guide makes all the difference.

When we're confused or feeling low, or when our sisters are, His Word clarifies and comforts. "Every part of Scripture is God-breathed and useful one way or another—showing us truth, exposing our rebellion, correcting our mistakes, training us to live God's way. Through the Word we are put together and shaped up for the tasks God has for us" (2 Tim. 3:16–17 Message).

Let's be Yes Sisters who remind one another of the power to identify and deal with the enemy's lies that can really mess with us. Lies that plague our thoughts—the ones that claim God doesn't see us or love us and no one else will either, and the ones that try to rob us of joy and hope.

We hold up God's Word to one another as our direction for life:

> The revelation of GOD is whole
> and pulls our lives together.
> The signposts of GOD are clear
> and point out the right road.
> The life-maps of GOD are right,
> showing the way to joy.
> The directions of GOD are plain and easy on the eyes. . . .
> God's Word warns us of danger
> and directs us to hidden treasure.
> Otherwise how will we find our way? (Ps. 19:7–9, 11–14
> Message)

Truth brings peace, even when that truth isn't easy to accept. Because honesty from a Yes Sister includes grace at its heart, we can handle it.

As for Janie, Shawna, and Gracie? God bless them for what they can teach us as well, such as how *not* to earn Yes Sister trust!

True Growth

Brielle and Carmen's story is based on real women's friendships. Carmen had to push through the defensiveness and self-protective habits that inhibited her. As a result, the growth she experienced from one lunchtime conversation began to change their friendship from the inside out, despite the new challenge of living far apart.

It's natural to feel awkward, intimidated, or even a little fearful when we receive truth from each other. But taking the risk to be honest with a trusted Yes Sister can transform us. Opening ourselves up in this way grows our humble strength. We learn how to handle reality productively and assertively. There's no overstating the impact those lessons have on our ability to be emotionally secure and create a safe environment for others to grow as well.

A woman who knows how to handle the truth is a force in this world. She is primed and ready for God to use her beyond her dreams.

A WORD FROM
a Yes Sister

Dr. Terry Whitt Bailey, *director of community development, city of Muncie, Indiana*

Embracing Tough Truth

It's not always easy to handle the truth. When people give us feedback or suggestions, we may see it as criticism rather than constructive feedback or loving advice.

I found myself reacting rather than responding to advice my friends and family were giving me when my husband suffered two strokes a couple of years ago. He lost the use of his left side, he lost his job, and he lost his ability to think and speak clearly.

I was working a full-time job and two part-time jobs to make ends meet and trying to take care of him as he lay in a hospital bed in our home. When my friends and family would ask how he was doing, I would give them the latest update on his prognosis. Then they would ask how I was doing, and I would respond that I was doing great.

But deep down I was broken and weary and keeping my emotions packed inside. People would tell me I looked tired and urge me to take care of myself, but I didn't know how to do that. It isn't uncommon for us, as caregivers, to develop a sense of denial and forget to take care of ourselves. There is too much to do for our loved one.

Then my best friend, Donna Armstrong, gave me a key to her house with instructions to meet her there after work. She arranged for me to spend the night while a home health aide cared for my husband. And she pampered me by feeding me, styling my hair, and sharing laughter and tears. I didn't realize how much I needed to have a moment when someone took care of *me*! People had been telling me to take care of myself, but they did not know how to help me do that. Donna knew I needed help—and that I needed permission and a push.

The Bible tells us this: "Let us not love with words or speech but with actions and in truth" (1 John 3:18). Donna helped me understand that the loving advice from my sister-friends was for not only my benefit but also my husband's benefit. I have given myself permission to take care of me, and now I help other caregivers do the same for themselves.

Chapter 15

We WILL Rise from the Ashes

> He has sent me to bind up the brokenhearted,
>   to proclaim freedom for the captives
> and release from darkness for the prisoners . . .
>   to comfort all who mourn . . .
> to bestow on them a crown of beauty instead of ashes.
>
> Isaiah 61:1–3

Several months have passed while this book has taken shape. Sunny summer days filled with brainstorming and outlining gave way to autumn colors and drafting chapter by chapter.

Another Thanksgiving is in the books. Firelight flickers in hearths across the miles, and cold temperatures call for cozy indoor moments. A new year beckons us to consider where we've been and what we'd like to do differently in the future.

During all this introspection, we add more wood to the fire. Soon drifts of ash like gray snow load the floor of the firebox. Later on, when the hearth has cooled, we must clear out the box.

One exhale into its unlit interior sends a poof of debris flying. We watch the dead particles hover, linger, then slowly sink. The cloud clears as the ash accumulates once more at the bottom.

Ash is the detritus of flame-destroyed trees. Those trees stood tall and alive in earlier days. They drew sustenance from the earth. They reached for the sky and offered a haven beneath their canopy. Now ashes are all that remain.

The nos of our lives can accumulate like ash. Our singed hopes languish in drifts around us. The slightest wind casts the burnt bits of our spirit so far away that we don't hold out hope of recapturing any of it.

We don't have much use for ash. We discard it. If only we could draw one more spark from it, one flicker of promise.

But life can't come from death.

Can it?

Life from Death

Ashes have long symbolized grief, mourning, and loss. Ancient cultures mourned with sackcloth and ashes, which are the by-product of destruction. They form when something has been charred, scorched, branded, blistered, cauterized, parched, scalded, seared, or singed. Something must be wrecked, ended, to make an ash heap.

I'm reminded of old Dickens stories set in nineteenth-century London. I can replay scenes of impoverished characters dressed in ragged clothing, filthy with ashes and soot, as they yearn for reprieve. In the classic *A Christmas Carol*, smoldering ashes in the fireplace do nothing to warm the office of Ebenezer Scrooge, where poor Bob Cratchit shivers as he works.

Ashes don't conjure jovial images. At best they make life gray, and who wants a gray life?

But those gray, good-for-nothing ashes have hidden benefits like these:

1. Ashes repel slugs and snails in the garden.
2. Ashes work as a road and sidewalk deicer without harming concrete.
3. Ash-and-water paste makes a nontoxic silver polish.
4. Ashes soaked in water make lye, a key ingredient in home-made soap.
5. For plants that love calcium-rich soil, ash mixed into the soil during planting boosts the plant's health.
6. The potassium in ash slows algae's growth in a pond by strengthening the other plants.

As much as it surprises us, something burned-out, dull, and void of vitality can still have purpose—life beyond its deadness.

How does that help us catch a fresh vision of the potential lying dormant in the ashes of our lives, those parts of us that feel stalled or even ended by the nos?

Words like *consumed*, *annihilated*, *broken*, *demolished*, *devastated*, *blighted*, *wasted*, *ravaged*, *shattered*, and *ruined* hold an air of finality, of endings. They tell of the past, of things that are over and done and unrecoverable.

But God sees ash-heap words differently. They speak of opportunities for Him to reveal Himself in their midst. They are ready for His breath of rebirth.

He ended death for us through the gift of His Son, Jesus. He created us for eternity, and even when we destroyed that future, God said no to that end and created a new beginning.

The nos that have hit you may have been deaths of one sort or another. Any significant loss or disappointment can trigger grief that takes time to work through. Waves of sorrow and regret can feel powerful enough to take us down, even bury us in an ash pile of defeat.

But let's never stop reminding one another that God—the only one who can raise the dead—changes everything. Hear His yes to you. Death wanted to be final. Satan wanted to overrun God and turn all of creation to drifts of devastation. But God dealt the enemy a resounding no so we could accept His yes.

As your Yes Sister throughout this book, I've been encouraging you to focus on God. He not only puts ashes to good use but also fills them with His glory and shines it inside of you. He invites you to bring your sorrows and exchange them for the joy He offers.

He creates new life in and for you. In fact, birthing new life from what was dead is the grandest theme of His Word to us. That new life He desires to work in you *will* impact the here and now, the everyday, the little and big issues.

The Best Is Yet to Come

You can rise from the ashes. The renewed you can be better than before life turned to ash. Your impact as a Yes Sister will be directly and profoundly charged with the power you gained from your own rise from loss. When you experience God and your Yes Sisters pulling you through, you won't ever be the same again. Your personal story equips you to speak truth into someone else. She will learn through you that her loss of a job or someone she depended on or a home where she found sanctuary is not the end.

In the musical *The Greatest Showman*, the main character, Phineas Barnum, goes from rags to riches and then is headed for rags again when his building burns to the ground. The ashes and soot that cover everything cast bleakness over the future for his family and his employees.

But that destruction creates a new starting point for him. He has recently come to understand that he wasted decades chasing after what wouldn't truly fulfill him, and it nearly cost him what really matters. Out of the ashes that signify so much loss, his life becomes deeper and richer.

Can ashes serve a useful purpose in our growing process as "oaks of righteousness, a planting of the Lord for the display of his splendor" (Isa. 61:3)?

Yes, yes, and *YES*.

The verses from Isaiah that opened this chapter lead to a renewed purpose revealed later in Isaiah 61.

After God recreated and restored and granted a crown of beauty instead of ashes, He gave a new plan: "They will rebuild the ancient ruins and restore the places long devastated; they will renew the ruined cities that have been devastated for generations" (Isa. 61:4).

And he gives us a rebuilding role as a Yes Sister to others. We get to be part of His creation of new life. That's a gift with awe-inspiring return blessings. The Creator of the universe designed the yes of a Yes Sister to play a key part in His redemptive story, which He started writing long ago.

Out of the Ashes

I've experienced times when I've been on my knees praying desperately for God's help. I've cried until I fell into an exhausted sleep. I've wondered if I'd ever feel happy again. You may have felt that way too.

The hardest times often become the seasons that bind us closer as Yes Sisters than the seasons of plenty.

When we nurture Yes Sister relationships, we don't face those tough moments alone. We have prayer warriors, encouragers, and people to pick up our child from school, send an encouraging note, and make us get out of bed when we don't want to or climb into bed beside us and hold us while we cry.

Yes Sisters won't just tell us we will rise up; they will cheer us on as we do. They will remind us of our greater purpose. They will inspire us to trust fully in God's tender and understanding care of our hearts.

Brenda found Yes Sisters for a season in a Bible study. Several of the women, including her, were in the middle of faith crises that left them wondering if God's best for them had already passed. Was His plan for them to endure those same battles for the rest of their lives?

Brenda dared to be real and asked her sisters for help with her toughest challenges. Scriptural declarations from women who had fought their way through similar doubts helped her stay the course.

One of Brenda's sisters, Abby, introduced the hurting women to Isaiah 61, a chapter that supports all the encouragement we humans can offer to anyone in a tough spot.

God wastes nothing. He uses every bit of the debris for our good and so that we extend His life-giving love to others. This is the most profound work of a Yes Sister, and it happens very often through that hated pile of discarded ashes.

Here are a few more reminders to help you focus on the good yet to come. You can pass these suggestions along to others as you live as a Yes Sister:

1. Trust God more deeply today than yesterday. Take the risk to trust more (Jer. 17:7–8).
2. Imagine God asking you, "Will you defend who I say I am?" and "Will you defend who I say you are?" Trust His heart of love even (especially) when you can't understand His path (Gen. 17:1; 26:24; Exod. 15:26; 34:6; Isa. 41:10; 43:13; 46:9).
3. Do not fear. "The LORD will fight for you; you need only to be still" (Exod. 14:14). See also Deuteronomy 3:22.

4. God will redeem losses (Jer. 31:3–4; Joel 2:18–27).

5. Train your thoughts to view every setback as God preparing you for what He knows is coming in your future (Gen. 50:20).

6. God often led His people through wilderness training, and it always led to something—to *the* assignment, *the* fit for that person (think of Moses, the apostle Paul, Jesus).

7. Make a Scripture pillow. Use fabric markers to write your favorite Scripture verses on it. Rest your thoughts each night on God's truth, hope, love, and life.

8. Raise your Ebenezer in remembrance of what God has done. First Samuel 7 tells of a time when God won a great battle for His people. Samuel the prophet raised a stone of Ebenezer and said, "Thus far the LORD has helped us" (v. 12). Isaiah 46:9 says, "Remember the things I have done in the past. For I alone am God!" (NLT).

You can rise again! Believe it today more than you did yesterday. God will bless your faith. Your Yes Sisters will remind you of that.

A WORD FROM
a Yes Sister

Genma Holmes, entrepreneur, writer, radio host

A Light-Bulb Moment

As a clone of my mother, my grandmother, and the aunts who influenced and shaped my life, I had the true superwoman complex. I often helped others mend their hearts and minds, and I offered advice to businesses. But until life hit me in the face, I didn't realize that I didn't allow others to share their wisdom or fruits with me.

I was face-palmed when a marketing deal I had worked on night and day for almost a year, one that would earn me two thousand dollars, went south.

I sat in a corner bawling and wondering why this had happened to me. Teary-eyed and snotty-nosed, I shared my predicament with a dear friend. She listened with hearing ears and gave me advice that helped me grow up and learn the business of business.

She said, "You have a gift of bringing people together because you see a bigger picture when we all work together. Your heart is always pure, and you assume everyone will be fair and honest. But you must learn to ask for your portion before the deal is brokered and understand the power of a contract. Until you learn to value your portion and the skills you bring to the table, you will feel used and angry. And this will continue to happen."

That was a light-bulb moment for me that has been shining brightly ever since. I have sought her counsel on many business endeavors since that time. My two-grand disappointment was a hard lesson I will always cherish. It took a sister-friend to help me see that devaluing what I bring to the table undermines the gifts God gave me.

PART 3

More
of Yes

Chapter 16

Becoming a Yes Sister

Now, like infants at the breast, drink deep of God's pure kindness.
Then you'll grow up mature and whole in God.

1 Peter 2:2 Message

Picture the sweetness of a bright-eyed little girl seated at her mother's makeup table. She gazes into the mirror, angles her head this way and that to ensure she completely covered her cheeks. Those cheeks, still baby-fat round and silky-soft kissable, are smeared with a mixture that could be equal parts blush and leftover jelly from lunch.

Perfume clogs the air like a clingy flowering vine. You try not to sneeze or otherwise noticeably react. She's in a world of her own, a world of innocence and dreams, not to be disturbed.

A floppy sun hat sits too big and cockeyed atop her untamed mane like an unspoken testament to her carefree heart.

Several necklaces are draped around her neck. The few she left behind spill in a tangled mess from her mother's jewelry box. Bracelets clink awkwardly on her wrists, so she shoves them farther up her arms where they fit better. They can't get in the way as she generously applies crimson lipstick. Yes, ma'am, she knows just how to do it.

She sets down the lipstick tube and regards the vision she created. Her red mouth widens in a satisfied grin. She knows she is THE. MOST. LOVELY.

We can only agree.

She stands and spins around the room, then stops abruptly at the entrance to Mom's closet. Her eyes widen.

"Shoes!" she squeals. Twice.

High heels—they're everywhere! They were neatly lined up. But in a moment, all except one pair (black patent stilettos) lie scattered over the closet floor. Her eye for great shoes foreshadows the healthy bit of sass she'll wear through her teen years.

She teeters on small feet that fill half the heels, then steadies herself by grabbing on to a nearby shelf—one that holds an array of handbags. Of course, she must have one of those. A pink leather satchel ought to be just right for the office or "to run erins" like Mom does.

She's fresher to this world than we are, but like you and me, she has a one-of-a-kind story that is breathtaking and purposeful. She was created to grow and thrive.

We, the little girl's virtual Yes Sisters, want to protect her so that nothing crushes her beautiful spirit during the challenges, heartaches, and stresses to come.

She has much to learn of matters beyond outward appearance, so much to understand about being a woman and a Yes Sister.

It's our role to show her. She needs our example of what it means to be whole, vibrant, empowered, giving, and tenacious in hope. She needs to learn that those enduring qualities grow through humility, surrender, obedience, and full-hearted devotion to her Maker.

She needs older Yes Sisters to pave the way by consistently reaching for the *best* abundant blessings for ourselves and for others. It's okay, good even, that she realizes we aren't perfect. She needs to know more importantly that we are committed to helping one another through it all.

We need to keep growing as Yes Sisters, not only for each other but also so that little girl can learn how to become a Yes Sister for the next girl.

●●●

What is it about playing dress-up that appeals to so many little girls? Is it the anticipation of growing older? The hope of being beautiful like Mom and other women? Visions of the glorious "what ifs" the future may hold?

We'll never stop carrying part of our girlhood selves inside of us. Age doesn't mean we lose our love for creating and embodying beauty. Nor do we stop wanting to be capable and respected and, most of all, loved. And we will never stop longing for connection, to be known and accepted in our authenticity.

But we are always changing. If we stop growing, we don't remain steady at a certain level of "aliveness" forever. We stagnate and inevitably take backward steps.

Stagnation results not so much from the mistakes we make, but more often from being numbed by life's distractions. Unmet expectations. Busyness that leads to exhaustion, disappointments that pile up as discouragement, the temptation to compare ourselves with others only to come up wanting—those sidetracks drain our interest in life's most important pursuits.

The best pursuits draw us closer to God and welcome Him into every area of our lives. He inspires us to live each moment to its fullest, confident that He empowers us for His purposes and committed to growing as effective, influential women.

There will never be a day on this earth when you and I won't depend on God's life-breath. The fullness (or lack) of His life in us impacts how we develop as effective Yes Sisters.

Close-Up View of the Big Picture

A friend recently shared her frustrations about the fickleness of aging eyesight. For years, her prescriptions didn't change much for both eyes. She was used to ordering contacts each year—the left side for distance and the right side for close up—and keeping a pair of progressive-lens glasses handy at night. *Easy peasy.*

But then her midforties arrived and complicated her simple routine. Reading glasses became a constant accessory, either on her face or on top of her head. Managing it all became cumbersome, especially the eye drops, solutions, and cases involved. When summer meant adding sunglasses to the jumble, she figured there had to be a better solution.

After trying multiple things over a couple of years, she finally settled on the best she and her eye doctor could do. Since her job involved a great deal of computer work, it made sense to choose the optimal contact prescription for close-up work. That meant losing the reading glasses but gaining a pair of distance glasses for driving. Plus, by then, her progressive lenses needed to be replaced since they were no longer great for either close-up *or* far away.

She joked that it might have been simpler (and less pricey) to carry a pair of binoculars instead! Depending on which end she looked through and how she tweaked the focus, they'd allow her to see either long-range or close-up.

Becoming an effective Yes Sister works a little like binoculars. We may have to adjust our focus to really see the people in our close, everyday circle. Family, friends, coworkers, the mail carrier, bus drivers, teachers, neighbors, the grocery clerk—every one of them harbors some kind of wound or regret. Not everyone takes the time or invests the effort to look deeper, to pay attention to close-up details that reveal what's going on behind another person's façade. Everyone is dealing with more than what she talks about or the highlights she shares on social media.

Unless we're proactive about it, we're bound to overlook opportunities to make a difference for someone. The homes in our neighborhoods have closed doors and windows covered with blinds that hide what's going on behind them. Those barriers keep from our view the heartache, disillusionment, and desperation, and make it possible to live withdrawn, isolated, unseen, and unknown lives. Let's help spare each other that emptiness.

On the flip side, keeping a broad, hope-beyond-this-moment view in mind also takes deliberateness. How easy is it to spend an entire day wrapped up in our own thoughts and to-dos of the present moment?

When we are blinded by our own concerns, we become limited to a narrow awareness of the world. Or we become consumed with the immediacy of *now* and *right here* to the point that we forget the eternal perspective God operates from across the globe. He never loses sight of His grand plan of redemption that impacts the whole of humanity. At the same time, He's always close-up and present for each of us.

We mature as Yes Sisters when we encourage one another to look deep, look up, and keep our focus trained around us so we don't miss opportunities to spread hope near and far, personally and globally.

Always Becoming

Who taught you what it means to be a woman? What characteristics does she embody? Does her lifestyle and do her choices match up with what she claims? If they don't, you've probably already decided not to follow her lead.

Even if your list of Yes Sisters is short, your story still gives you a certain amount of wisdom, which is needed to give close-up and wide-lens attention to what's going on in the lives of those around us. You even gain insights from the women who *haven't* faithfully been there for you.

A woman who grew up without a loving mother has unique perspectives and insights to pass along to a younger woman struggling with grief, healing, acceptance, forgiveness, and holding on to the truth of God's love for her.

One simple way to move forward as a Yes Sister is to recall your early influencers and communicate the impact they've made on your life. Let each of those women know that her investment in you continues to multiply.

Ask her what prompted her to reach out to you. What moved her heart to work on your behalf? Beyond compassion or empathy, what nudged her into action as a Yes Sister for you? What did she gain in return?

The Bible offers examples of women who influenced those around them. Elizabeth led the way for Mary when they were both pregnant (Luke 1:39–45). Lydia was a businesswoman who managed her family and helped others (Acts 16:14–15). We all have much to offer younger women who are seeking wise advice. If you feel called to be the more experienced, mentor kind of Yes Sister, consider these guidelines:

- Listen more than you speak, especially at first. Someone who feels heard is more likely to open up and trust you.
- Understand that younger generations experience life from a different perspective than you do. Try using their world for context, and envision yourself with your similar challenges but lived out in a framework that may make those challenges harder, easier, or even weirder for them than they were for you at the same stage.

- Advice can sound like criticism. Offer it sparingly, when the woman asks or welcomes it.
- Encourage, lift up, and show interest in what the younger woman can offer. Affirm her potential.
- Pay attention to the younger woman's strengths and help her discover what they are. She may not recognize them herself.
- A mentor is held up as an example. Work hard to live honorably, with integrity. It speaks volumes.
- Older women benefit in many ways from the joy, insights, and exuberance of a younger Yes Sister. Bless her by welcoming the ways she attempts to bless you.

We're all works in progress. Some days we're stronger than others. The "becoming" part of sisterhood never stops. We're either growing or stagnating. Practice keeps us growing.

Today is a good day to continue becoming.

A WORD FROM
a Yes Sister

Cynthia Ruchti, *author, speaker, literary agent, and the woman who said "YES!" to Angelia's desire to tell her story*

Yes Sister Beginnings

Jackie "spoke into my life." What does that mean? She invested in me. She poured into me. What does *that* mean? Whatever it is, she did it. She's a Yes Sister I've known for more than forty years.

Moving to the country as the mom of a toddler and a baby on the way, I was unprepared for how the blessings of country living came packaged with a radical dose of isolation. Unless the driver of one of the gravel trucks peeling down the road in front of our house waved at me while I waited to cross to our mailbox, I could go for days without seeing another human being. Don't judge, but I resorted to talking to the squirrels, chipmunks, and deer who called our acreage their home too.

Even as an introvert who can pull off a reasonable facsimile of extrovertedness when necessary, I longed for a friend. Prayed for a friend to do life with. Prayed . . . for . . . years.

I found out later that my nearest neighbor—a quarter of a mile away—was peppering heaven with the same prayer: "Send me someone, God, who can be my best friend." God answered our prayers with *each other*.

Our friendship hadn't seemed a natural fit at first. Jackie was watching her kids make their way through high school. She also worked nights and was twenty-two years older than I was, just two years younger than my mother.

Nonetheless, my kind and generous neighbor became more than a neighbor the day she said yes; she became a wonderful confidante and sister in the Lord. I had infrequently been in her home, but one day while returning something I'd no doubt borrowed, I saw a book of worship songs on her antique piano. I didn't ask, "Do you play the piano?" I asked, "Do you . . . do you love Jesus?"

Her *yes!* drove deep into my heart. Our budding friendship escalated from that moment of discovering the most important common ground two friends can know.

She mentored me in faith and raising children. For years, we prayed together every Friday afternoon for what started out as a half hour and blossomed into two hours or more. I taught her a few things I knew. We walked beside each other through innumerable challenges. As only God could orchestrate, together we produced a radio broadcast that started infinitesimally small and, eventually, grew to air on forty-eight stations. As we matured together, we spoke a steady stream of yeses over each other. "Yes, I'll be there for you." "Yes, I'm praying." "Yes, you can do this. How can I help?" "Yes, God is using you to bless others. You're blessing me."

Our age difference was obvious only on the surface. We'd become BFFs before that term was a thing.

The radio broadcast retired in 2012 after thirty-three continuous years on the air. Our Yes Sister status will not retire until one of us breathes our last breath. Decades difference between us? We hadn't noticed.

Now as I write and speak, she peppers heaven with her prayers for me. "What time will you be speaking? What time zone is that? I'm already praying, but I want to pray you through." Even while watching ninety approach as if it's in a hurry, she searches the Bible and her vast collection of books to create specific encouragement for me every time I teach or speak.

Because she no longer lives a cornfield away, we set up an appointment to talk by phone the day before I leave for an event. She literally speaks those encouraging words over me, pours into me, invests in me—and I in her—before we spend time together in prayer, thanking the One who answered our request for a Yes Sister.

It all started with a timely—and timeless—yes.

Chapter 17

The Yes Sisters You've Never Met

And may the Lord make you increase and abound in love for one another and for all.

1 Thessalonians 3:12 ESV

Whether you love airports or hate them, they're wonderful places to mix with people from all walks of life. Where better to meet or observe strangers from all seven continents? An airport is a people watcher's paradise.

It doesn't take long in a crowded airport to cross paths with

- business people zipping by, focused and distracted all at once;
- uneasy travelers rechecking their watches, luggage, phones, boarding passes, and the departure board;
- bored frequent flyers in food lines, their usual orders on the tip of their tongues;
- parents on business trips managing at-home issues on their phones;

- children bouncing around frazzled moms and dads;
- teenagers snapping gum, earbuds in place, with their gaze focused on the distance;
- travelers leaving home sad or excited; and
- travelers heading home relieved or uncomfortable.

People from every religion, ethnicity, and family history can be found there. Airports also serve up reminders that Yes Sisters around the globe are waiting for you to meet them.

It's a Big World, After All

When Clara moved across the country with her husband during the wagon-train days, she knew she would likely never see her mother, sisters, or friends again. They promised to keep in touch and tried. But a letter mailed on the second of April might arrive late in the fall. If at all. In 1843, distance meant separation in ways our technologically connected world can't comprehend.

The internet, cell phones, email, social media, video calls—none of those modern communication luxuries existed. A rocket hadn't zoomed to the moon. Satellites weren't orbiting and taking pictures of our faraway earth. Now it's simple to search online for an address anywhere in the world and zoom in for a close-up photo! Who would've imagined that would one day be possible a hundred, or even twenty, years ago? What did *online* mean, anyway? Hanging the clean laundry outside to dry?

We're able to connect with other people groups more now than ever in history. It's made this world so much more accessible.

We "meet" through blogs and online magazines, websites, and webinars. We catch a glimpse into other people's lives and cultures. We do daily life with women who live fifty or five thousand miles from us. We can duplicate Grandma's sour cream coffee cake recipe by watching her make the cake in a video call, in real time, in her home six states away. Or in France.

We can do more than imagine what life is like for women in faraway places. We read about their lives, talk to them, visit them, encourage and are encouraged by them. We connect.

Whose writings have inspired you? Is there a quote or piece of art or a celebrity or the face of a woman in need on the other side of the world whose story has found its way into your heart? Maybe a woman's comments on your mutual friend's social media piqued your curiosity to know that stranger better. If your friend was drawn to her, maybe you'd bond with her too.

When getting to know a Yes Sister, commonalities are a bonus, but they aren't necessary. We may have to look deeper to discover them. Our circumstances might be the polar opposite of a soon-to-be Yes Sister in a foreign land, and we may not even understand a word each other is saying because we speak different languages. But we share the yearning for friendship and for hope beyond our struggles. We're all created to bond with others.

A woman living in a lice-infested cardboard hut in a Honduran barrio longs for connection with other women as much as we do in the developed world. She needs the power of a personal yes with her name on it, a concept that may be as foreign to her as you and I are. An adolescent girl carrying water for her family in Africa needs life-changing hope as much as our daughters do. And the young woman in Thailand who is doing all she can to keep herself and her little sisters safe from human traffickers needs freedom from fear. We do, too, even if our fears are based on different troubles.

Often our deepest struggles unite us—which could be one of the hardest and most surprising blessings God provides us. God will put His fingerprints all over our search for Yes Sisters when we commit it to Him. Our hopes can't out-dream Him.

Try reading the following verses from a fresh viewpoint, as if He's writing specifically to us as women in search of or becoming Yes Sisters. He desires that we hold each other's hearts with the love and esteem we've received from Him.

> I came so they can have real and eternal life, more and better life than they ever dreamed of. (John 10:10 Message)

When we help one another discover the abundance God has planned for us, we experience the miracle of understanding more about who Jesus is. As we understand more, we find ourselves investing more time and energy to helping other women discover Him.

> For as the sky soars high above earth,
>   so the way I work surpasses the way you work,
>   and the way I think is beyond the way you think. (Isa.
>   55:9 Message)

Again, His yes is bigger than our own. Nothing—not geography or cultural boundaries nor religious differences nor age—can limit His ways of connecting women to one another.

> What marvelous love the Father has extended to us! Just look at it—we're called children of God! (1 John 3:1 Message)

God's yes guides us into knowing Him as our unfailing Dad. He reaches out His love toward us, inviting us to be His much-loved daughters and heirs of His creation.

> Don't shuffle along, eyes to the ground, absorbed with things right in front of you. Look up, and be alert to what is going on around Christ—that's where the action is. See things from his perspective. (Col. 3:1–2 Message)

Those verses from Colossians are like our battle cry as we fight for one another and the women we don't know yet. That's truly what this life is—a calling of epic, eternal magnitude in which every woman can play her own special role.

Making Connections

So how do we connect with a woman who could be a future Yes Sister? We aren't always near enough to invite her for coffee or serve together on a committee. We may not cross paths at work or church or in a gathering of moms at a playdate.

Here are a few ideas to jump-start broader thinking about how to keep expanding your community of Yes Sisters:

1. Read widely about topics that stir your mind, heart, and vision—women in ministry, military service, teaching, volunteering, foster care parenting. You're sure to find ways to reach out and help. Research and familiarize yourself with the greatest needs in undeveloped or war-torn countries and relief organizations already in place in those areas. Tapping in to sources already in action is a great way to connect and discover your niche. Maybe you're best fit to help the ones in need. Or maybe your specialty is serving those who serve.

2. Listen to meaningful podcasts that inspire women to live purposefully. Feeding yourself motivational, life-giving words helps keep you looking up and out at what's going on in the world. It prevents you from settling into too small of a world.

3. Sample a webinar. These offer comfortable, cost-effective ways to broaden your mind about topics that interest you.

Some of them may also provide interaction between participants. Every connection can prove to be valuable.

4. Consider yourself a lifelong learner. Learning is a passion that develops compassion and empathy, inspires a heart to reach out, and prevents stagnation. The world provides an endless supply of discoveries. Yes Sisters keep learning!

5. Write to women you admire and tell them how they've encouraged you. This goes for Yes Sisters who've built into you, as well as women you don't even know who have stood out to you. I've told you about my friend Sherrell, who sent me flowers and encouraging notes without having ever met me in person. I've never forgotten how much her proactive positivity meant to me. I've developed friendships through my work and been able to offer a number of women unique opportunities as interns or employees without knowing them beforehand. It's quite possible I've been more blessed than they have been.

A face-to-face relationship may be ideal, but the influence of sisters we'll never meet in person can impact us in refreshing ways.

You can be that influential sister for someone else too. The feeling that there's more to life than what you're experiencing isn't coincidence. God has great purpose for you and may be telling you that women are waiting to meet *you*, to hear *your* yes to them. Grab on and go with it, and prepare yourself for sweet relationships to come.

A WORD FROM
a Yes Sister

Maurita Sutton Brown, *PhD candidate in psychology*

Believing without Seeing

When I think about a Yes Sister I've never met, Bea Baylor comes to mind.

Someone who shares our beliefs and affirms our dreams is one of life's great treasures. Bea is that person for me. I have always been a dreamer and a planner. I oftentimes catch myself needing another woman's opinion or outlook on ideals I am working on. As a life coach, I desire an advisor as well.

I've traveled the world, educated myself to the level of a doctoral candidate, and built businesses. And I value my Yes Sister Bea to advise me about my chosen interests.

I remember my first encounter over the phone with her. I could not believe a woman I had never met could believe in me and my desires and then encourage me to complete them.

When Bea came into my life, I was about to make a decision that would change my entire journey with my family and business. Even though she lives in another state, she was there for me, listening and reasoning with me on godly decisions. She gave me life nuggets, and I received them all. She is an entrepreneur and business consultant, yet she finds the time to be one of my Yes Sisters.

I value her love and advice as we help each other accomplish our dreams. The most important part of our relationship is that we're comfortable enough to talk for hours, share business ideals, and laugh at what makes us who we are. I adore my Yes Sister I've never met (face-to-face)!

Chapter 18

Knowing and Forgiving the No Sisters

And above all these put on love, which binds everything together in perfect harmony. And let the peace of Christ rule in your hearts, to which indeed you were called in one body. And be thankful.

Colossians 3:14–15 ESV

It's time to talk about the "mean girl."

You know her. She and her gal pals have skulked the halls of every school without skipping a single generation. She might have fake smiled to your face before she stomped on your heart—usually in front of an audience of peers. Or she may have foregone the niceties, false or not, and sneered at you across the classroom for no apparent reason. She carried an air of authority and privilege. For some reason, she didn't like you. Putting you down made her feel better about herself (at least that's what her subconscious had convinced her).

In reality, she felt threatened, either by you or because you symbolized something to her about her own hurts or weaknesses.

Wow, Angelia, you might be thinking. *Way to encourage positivity and empowerment with this topic!*

I admit that calling the mean girl to mind probably doesn't elicit good emotions. Even now, years later, with life experience and maturing behind you, a reminder of her can affect you. Believe me, I get it.

Before we go on, take a deep breath. We're in this together, you and I. In this chapter, we're going to tackle the mean girl.

I mean, we're going to put her in her place.

No, that's not it either.

Sigh.

How about this? Let's work on forgiving her. (And maybe forgiving her will relieve you of those conflicting yet very human feelings that want her to pay for her wrongs.)

Whose face comes to mind when you think of a mean girl? Does your breath catch? Your heart miss a beat? Maybe the memory of her triggers anxiety or shame or still makes your blood boil.

Some girls in gymnastics cross my mind. So do a few women I've known over the years who chronically left the *constructive* out of "constructive criticism," and the ones who thought that using biting sarcasm toward me was funny. I've also crossed paths with my share of would-be friends who proved to have their own best interests at heart behind their flattering words.

It's ironic how writing a book about women who speak life and yes to my life has me revisiting memories of all the girls who did the opposite.

It's time for us to address our antagonists, those girls or women in our story who could have enjoyed our friendship but instead cast us off as unworthy. Laying aside old hurts unlocks the chains of unforgiveness, which only keep *us* bound, not *her*.

If we spin those hurts for our good and use the experiences to empower us for impactful Yes Sister living, each of our antagonists offers us valuable growth opportunities. The mean girls taught us crucial truths about people. Their actions illuminated the wonder of Jesus's love—and the uplift of Yes Sister love.

Take that, mean girls!

The fact that mean girls weren't limited to only my childhood proves that some don't shed their talons as they age. Instead, they refine and sharpen them into gel-painted, shiny-on-the-outside weapons of womanhood. A few of those "gems" I met later in life were like taller versions of the ones I knew when I was younger. They hauled their backpacks full of cruelties right on into adulthood.

You may work with one of them. Or she may be the mother of your daughter's BFF.

Or perhaps you remember acting like her a time or two, which may not be your proudest moments. Sin creates the capacity for meanness in each of us.

A No Sister?

Do you think referring to those mean girls as any sort of sister is a stretch? Is it possible to think of them as No Sisters?

These questions launch my thinking. The more I ponder, the more I value the oxymoronic term "No Sister."

We've considered so much already about the nos from which we're fighting our way back. Nos and No Sisters have brought us to our knees and shredded our hearts and our self-esteem. They've shamed us, lied to us, and held us back. They've turned others against us. They've embarrassed, frightened, teased, mocked, manipulated, humiliated, broken, and possibly even destroyed us. The faithfulness of sisterhood can't possibly have anything to do with nos.

That might be true if it weren't for a single word that changes everything: *redemption*. That's the big *R*—Jesus Redemption.

The apostle Paul wasn't technically a Yes Sister, but his story illustrates that relationship restoration is possible. Before redemption got hold of him, he (Saul at the time) was famous for pummeling people with the ultimate no: "No, you can no longer live. I am out to destroy you. And I'm justified in doing so." But his victims had done nothing wrong to him. Most didn't even know him. And none of his victims would have guessed the turnaround God would work in him.

When Jesus introduced himself to Saul in a shocking way, Saul could not remain the same toxic person. He did not change himself, however—that would have been impossible. The Holy Spirit proved mightier than all of Saul's sins and transformed a darkened heart into a redeemed soul who went on to speak and write more about Jesus's yeses for hurting human beings, more about love and compassion and truth, than any other person of his day. His example and his teaching on those subjects remain among the most widely read in history.

No Sisters can be called that because the juxtaposition of those two words—*no* and *sisters*—puts redemption in front of us every time we read them. Someone who symbolizes no to us can become a sister because redemption makes a 180-degree turn possible. And redemption is the victor over every hurt you and I carry.

A no girl or woman can become a sister. The mean girl is a broken soul. She hurts others out of her own hurt and sinful nature. We claim the Holy Spirit's victory every time we see her through Jesus's eyes and pray for restoration on her behalf.

No Sisters are not our real enemies. Satan is the enemy of their souls, same as ours. He wants more than anything to twist our thoughts to believe that redemption and forgiveness of a No Sister is a ridiculous, impossible idea.

Remembering our true enemy keeps us from wasting precious energy fighting against imperfect people, which is the lesser fight.

After all, it's energy from our own unhealed heart we're fighting with, so it isn't efficient or productive like the energy that comes from forgiving a persecutor.

Is it possible to forgive our persecutors? Absolutely, but not without the Holy Spirit's power. Only He can free us from unforgiveness toward a No Sister. We need His redemption as much as she does.

When a No Sister crosses our minds, we can allow Jesus's love for her and His desire for her redemption to overcome our feelings about anything she did or could do to us. When that happens, we enjoy a new level of healing.

In Him, we win. And what's more, we even begin to want Him to redeem *her* brokenness so she can experience healing too.

Releasing Our Wounds

As strange as it sounds, I've discovered the potential for healing by working through forgiving myself for being a victim. *Please hear me clearly: the need to forgive ourselves is not because we were in the wrong for being on the receiving end of mistreatment.* This kind of forgiveness releases us from bondage to someone else's bad decisions or harmful actions.

It isn't uncommon for us to treat our past self harshly and take on blame for being victimized. Our wounds hurt personally because we've been struck in vulnerable areas. Those hits create an environment ideal for lies to take root in our minds. Over time, if we don't combat the lies of unworthiness and shame, feelings of weakness and despair, they become a twisted version of truth in our lives.

One powerful method to confront the lies that continue to victimize us involves confronting them with spiritual truth. By doing so, we forgive ourselves and find freedom from the misplaced burdens we carry.

By working through the steps of forgiving ourselves, we practice new habits of grace, claiming the truth that Jesus makes us wholly accepted and better equipped for our future.

Forgiveness releases us to live our fullest life.

In Person or Not

Some relationships with No Sisters may never improve. If someone isn't safe for you, don't assume you need to keep working at the relationship. Showing grace toward a toxic person requires healthy boundaries, like guardrails.

Can a Yes Sister help you work through an unhealthy relationship with a No Sister? The wise advice of a mentor sister who doesn't have the strong, reactive emotions you do about the situation may provide fresh perspective. And she can keep pointing you toward the far side of forgiveness, where you will enjoy its blessings.

But what if you're stuck in circumstances that don't allow you to distance yourself from the No Sister? If you live or work near her, or if she's family or you share mutual friends, you may face ongoing reminders and your paths may cross frequently. Proximity can complicate healing.

Sheneille was living her dream. She loved her family, her job, her life. But her world unraveled when she lost her dream job—and a steady financial future—to a coworker. The coworker, Diondra, twisted facts and damaged Sheneille's professional reputation, adding insult to injury. Sheneille struggled to find another position. She finally had to settle for a job outside the field she loved that didn't compare to what she lost financially.

What made the situation even more difficult was that the women lived around the corner from each other and had kids in the same school. Diondra posted about her career successes on social media. They shared a number of mutual contacts online. So as much as

Sheneille avoided social media to spare herself more painful reminders, she couldn't eliminate it. She needed the updates about her children's school, sports teams, and church events.

It hurts to lose a dream. The pain multiplies if a No Sister takes that dream. Sheneille lives with this ongoing reality every day. She can't get away from Diondra unless she uproots her family with no certainty that doing so would bring healing.

If you were a Yes Sister to someone in a situation similar to Sheneille's, how would you counsel that sister to rise above her loss and work toward healing? Consider these ideas:

- Limit exposure to the No Sister as much as possible.
- Create and maintain boundaries where possible.
- Do not give in to the self-destructive temptation to check the woman's social media sites or drive past her house to see what "having it all" must feel like. A No Sister does not have it all. She can't understand or experience real fulfillment or peace. Her life is hollow. However, you still can be filled and joyful in Jesus's presence.
- Don't ignore the possibility of a huge change. God may be nudging you toward a new blessing you can't have unless you leave an old dream in the past.
- Remember that a No Sister may act in control, but she is not. God is. A No Sister has no more control of life than you do.
- God will never blink and miss something you need Him to do. He will always be who you need most.

One more thought: give yourself a gift today. Let go of any expectation that a No Sister will meet you where you are. Assume that she can't, that she doesn't have the emotional or relational tools for it.

As one friend groaned, "I just want her to get it! Not 'get it,' as in a meteor crashing to earth and landing on her. I only wish she'd be honest and care how her actions hurt me."

It's a reasonable wish. But that, too, is God's to work on. Leave the No Sister to Him while He and you work on *you*. Life is so much more peaceful and joyful in His care. The positive steps you take are primarily for you. A No Sister may never get it. But your Lord and your Yes Sisters do.

A WORD FROM
a Yes Sister

Heidi Chiavaroli, *award-winning author*

Choosing Freedom

What she did consumed my every thought, my every moment.

I used to think forgiveness was easy. Before this. Before I had to forgive a sister in the faith who had hurt me deeply with both actions and words.

I became obsessed with the wrongness of what she'd done and the rightness of what I'd done. And I was absolutely *certain* that Jesus saw it my way.

Yet I was in chains. I cried often. I'd never felt so misunderstood, so alone. And the thought of forgiving? Well, that was almost more painful than the thought of how I'd been wronged.

I clung to my anger for weeks. I rehashed the events in my head. I talked God into being on my side (or so I thought).

Still, no peace.

I knew what God asked of me, but I wanted nothing to do with it. My anger festered until I felt a rotting in my spirit. It was ugly—I knew it, God knew it. And still, with the gentleness of a lamb, He called me from it.

The woman who'd wronged me never did ask for forgiveness. And yet I couldn't stand the wall between us—the hurt, the awkwardness. I reached out to her, slaying my pride and even asking for forgiveness for my part in the dispute. I did it because I couldn't take the ugliness corroding my heart any longer. I did it because Jesus asked me to.

The reward was immediate. A lightening in my spirit, a peace, a freedom, a knowing that a big God was at work in my small circumstances, that He wanted to grow me through them, that He really and truly intended what was best for me all along.

Chapter 19

Righting Wrong Yeses

But you, God, shield me on all sides;
    You ground my feet, you lift my head high;
With all my might I shout up to God,
    His answers thunder from the holy mountain.

Psalm 3:3–4 Message

We've spent eighteen chapters hailing the glories of a good yes. Is there such a thing as a wrong yes? Isn't that an oxymoron? After this deep of a look at the value of yes, we might assume all nos are the enemy of good.

From a different angle, we see that the best yeses include wisdom as part of their foundation. The best yeses are born of insight and thoughtfulness and discernment to know if the timing is God-blessed. The best yes can be spelled *n-o* for good reason.

Misplaced yeses can cause more trouble than they do to help. So we nurture habits to avoid them while still living as sisters who are all about the capital Y, best Yes.

When a No Is the Best Yes

Our emotions and motivations can partner and direct us well. Other times, not so much. Noticing that someone needs a yes can trigger the following responses from us:

- Compassion for her struggle
- Sympathy because we relate
- Guilt because we think we're supposed to operate with a helping heart and practice love in action, but something in us hesitates
- Desire to "be the change"
- Desire to do the most we can

We feel *compassion* because we don't like to see others in pain, especially when we could do something to ease it. But the enemy of our souls can twist our good intentions so masterfully that we're fooled. Our human nature isn't prone to moderation. We tend toward excess. However, an excess of misdirected compassion can make us into enablers. When we offer a wise yes, we practice supportive compassion that doesn't pity others or coddle their negative habits.

Memories of how lost we have felt prompts *sympathy* that can turn us into would-be fixers. But for a woman stuck in victim mode, overdone sympathy can encourage her to stay entrenched in that unhealthy state. A measured dose of sympathy in the context of our hope-filled outlook does more good for someone than helping her wallow.

A worm of *guilt* in our gut might convince us we're always meant to be the one to step up and invest in someone else. If we see a need, we're supposed to meet it, right? Not necessarily. We get in God's way when we jump in too quickly without pausing to consider the whole situation. If we always commit with a knee-jerk reaction, we could be distracted from a different yes He wants us to act on. Or we could rob someone else of an opportunity to be the yes. Or we could take on burdens of guilt that are misplaced and were never ours to carry. The enemy frequently uses the misplaced-guilt tactic to steer us wrong. We aren't God, so let's not guilt ourselves into trying to act like everyone's savior.

About that desire to "be the change". . . God does call us to live differently, unselfishly. We're not on Earth for our own good or to build our own castles. God has work to do, and we are ready and willing to help. But the temptation toward narcissistic altruism is real. It's very human to want to be noticed and validated, even for our generosity. We want to live with purpose.

But this good goal makes us vulnerable to pride's corruption, which is never far from most of our motivations. It's all too easy to feel successful in one area and then let pride morph into the belief that you're the only person capable of serving others who aren't quite as far along.

Many times this kind of situation is an invitation for God to help us learn humility!

A desire to be productive and *do the most we can* often fools us into thinking that more is better. Busyness can be a trap, a liability, a distraction, and even an idol. In our society, busyness is often viewed as a badge of honor. Even if we aren't big fans of our packed schedule, we tend to be tied to it anyway. Overcommitment can wreak havoc on the most well-intended yes.

Never in His Word does God ask us to make busyness king. He asks us to love Him and draw near to Him and abide in Him, the King. He calls us to accept His times of rest and to claim His peace that directs us inside and out. Then out of that filling, He asks us to love others.

We plumb the depths of our souls and His presence in the quiet. It's the same in our relationships with others—we most effectively hear them in the quiet. Busy living can limit the time we have to go deep, slow down, be quiet, and hear and truly listen to someone—as well as to God's direction about whether to say yes.

Are we honest enough with ourselves to recognize a subtle motivation that may be more about us than the beneficiary of our serving and giving?

Offering the Best Yes

God doesn't ask any of us to answer all the yeses. Not even the busy woman who is enlisted to do more and more because everyone knows she gets things done. Here are a few tips for discerning the best yes:

1. *Practice the pause.* When you're asked to do something or you sense a need you could help meet, pause before making a decision. Giving yourself time to think allows the idea and the scope of the commitment to register. It also provides time to ask God what He wants you to do and time to receive His answer. His Spirit provides you with the words to encourage someone, as well as the wisdom to know when to stay silent.
2. *"Let me think that over."* This is a fantastic default response. It sends the message that you intend to assess the need. If you end up saying yes, the person can expect that you will put the same thoughtfulness into the effort you offer and that you're prepared to do what's needed. If you say no, the person can rest easier knowing you didn't decide flippantly. It is not helpful to commit halfway or halfheartedly to someone who needs support that goes the distance.
3. *Priority checks.* These are ongoing and keep the focus on what's best, not merely on what's good. They come in handy when the demands of serving take over and become our master. God is God. Serving can grow toxic if it's given

godlike priority. If it takes our first and best resources away from being with Him or the ones He puts in our closest circle of care (such as immediate family and those depending on us), even a good deed done for good reasons may assume a godlike priority. Trouble born from misplaced priorities will catch up to us eventually.

If you're up to your neck in a commitment that you believe God is releasing you from or never meant for you to take on, begin with prayer and honesty. He can make up for your mistakes. There may be fallout to deal with, but He won't let someone else miss finding Him because of your error. Even our biggest mistakes can't cancel out God's plans for someone else.

It can also be good to ask for insights from your own Yes Sisters who might know a thing or two about a yes that we need to end.

The Yes Blessing of the Right No

How can we give someone a yes by telling her no? By saying no when it's someone else's time to be the yes. When that person is God, He wants us to get out of His way and let Him work. Practicing restraint until we have peace about our role shows wisdom.

Our best yes can come in the form of holding back from trying to fix something for another person if God wants her full attention. She's better off tucked away alone with Him for that season so she can see Him work. What we all need most is to experience His presence and power in our lives, even more than our very real need for a human support system.

Offering encouragement and remaining quietly available to listen may be what's needed. If He asks us to hold back and let Him work, that's also His urging to pray diligently.

No *can* be a God-blessed yes.

A WORD FROM
a Yes Sister

Amy Parker, *author*

The Best Yes

Once when I had made a commitment to volunteer for a ministry at a conference, I realized that the dates were the same as my family's upcoming fall break trip. The ministry only had three people to set up, present a breakout session, and staff the booth for three days. If I didn't show up, all of that work would fall to only two people. But I knew, without a doubt, that I had made the commitment to my family first, and I had to honor that commitment.

Cringing, I wrote a super apologetic email to this ministry team that I had grown to love. I felt horrible for making such a preventable mistake. The first member of the team to reply was the person I dreaded hearing from the most—one of the remaining two conference volunteers who was now going to be picking up my slack.

She immediately offered a plan B, adding, "Enjoy that family. They are precious."

Immediately, that huge boulder in my stomach dissolved. I realized that it's women friends like these who get us through life. It's the everyday forgiveness, everyday understanding, everyday encouragement to enjoy everyday moments that make up this lifetime of joy and success.

Chapter 20

Yes Sisters of the Bible

Your testimonies are my heritage forever,
for they are the joy of my heart.

Psalm 119:111 ESV

Rahab kept her face stoic as she passed the group of people gathered near the market. Relieved to be done with her shopping, she hurried in the direction of her home, away from the crowd. Most of the men and women were familiar to her, but she hadn't gotten to know any of them. And they knew only her reputation.

Before she was out of earshot, their words sliced into her.

"What is *she* doing here?"

"I can't believe she has the nerve to leave her house."

"I'm glad I didn't bring my children to town today."

"Do not look at her!"

Even though Rahab had heard the talk for years, the comments still cut deep. She held her head up but squeezed her eyes closed until the tears stopped gathering.

Within minutes, she'd returned to her front door. Fumbling with her purchases, she glanced around and was startled to see a dark form standing in the shadows of a tree down the path. He moved enough into the fading light to reveal himself and kept his focus on her. He was an older man she recognized. His clothing spoke of prestige and authority. A leering expression contorted his features. He, too, glanced around as if he didn't want to be seen.

Rahab hefted her burdens to one arm so she could grasp the door latch with her free hand. Anxious to get inside her home before he reached her, she gave him a curt shake of her head and locked the door behind her. She dropped her things at her feet and stilled her emotions. It did no good to give in to bitterness and self-pity.

You made your bed. Now you lie in it.

Although it was inaudible, the hiss of that familiar voice rattled her.

Long after Rahab fell asleep that night, a sharp knock woke her.

No. She rolled over and willed the person to leave her alone. There had to be another way.

But the caller was insistent. Every few seconds another sharp knock pelted her door. Finally, she pushed herself up off her bed and pulled up the shoulder of her nightgown to cover her skin. She wrapped a blanket around her thin body and answered the door.

● ● ●

We don't know Rahab, who is introduced in the book of Joshua, any more than the mean-spirited people who surrounded her knew her. She was a prostitute who said yes daily while living a life of no.

We can only guess what in her history brought her to the point of selling her body. She reminds us that behind every barrier of self-protection and bad life choice waits a wounded human being who is a complex blend of strengths and weaknesses, hurts and healing. Any of us can grow accustomed to negative responses from others, but that does nothing to reduce their impact. No one is ever unwoundable.

Rahab's story is chock-full of pain and heartache, sin and grace, lies and coping mechanisms, mistakes and regrets, desires for love and lingering hopes. The Bible doesn't give details, but the human heart hasn't changed. The effects of sin have chased all of creation since that terrible day in the garden.

We don't know whether Rahab's willful choices initiated her downfall, but chances are good that she'd been subjected to the hand of evil at some point. An emotionally and spiritually healthy, loved woman doesn't seek out that desperate lifestyle.

Even behind her closed door, Rahab could not get away from her hurts and sins. The sight of her no doubt prompted other women to holler, "No!" (to her as well as to their husbands, sons, and brothers).

But Rahab understood that God was about to do something big, and she wanted her story to become part of His story. She didn't know the scope of God's plan to deliver her hometown of Jericho to the Israelites. But God gave her enough understanding. She was ready. She wanted more. She wanted what was real. God knew her deepest yearnings, and He worked with perfect timing and precision to ready her for His purpose.

There were two callers knocking at her door that night—Israelite spies who meant her no harm and weren't there to use her. Their words brought the salvation she craved. Hiding them from the wicked authorities of her own people, Rahab aligned herself with the Lord.

Her life-changing trust echoes through history to us: "I know that the LORD has given you this land. . . . For the LORD your God is God in heaven above and on the earth below" (Josh. 2:9, 11).

With that, Rahab set her feet on the solid ground of God's holy yes for her. God called her out of a life of no, and she was paying attention. In fact, it's probable that the very nos that had marked her, the ones she wanted freedom from, were the tools God used to pique her spiritual sensitivity so she was able to recognize His call.

That night marked the turning point, not only for her but for an entire nation and for every human being in every generation since.

Rahab the former prostitute became an ancestor of Jesus and played a key role in His salvation promise. Because of her example, she became *our* ancient Yes Sister!

Which of her neighbors could have guessed that she, *that* woman, was God's hands and feet to help Him guide His people to the promise and fullness He'd been working toward for so long?

Would we have been tender enough to recognize that the Lord was working through her brokenness? He *adores* those who have grown accustomed to no, and He loves when we open our hearts enough to see what He will do.

God often works His most profound miracles through our most difficult, unlikely stories. Yes Sisters like Rahab pause and listen. Each individual yes changes history.

Esther

Esther was another unlikely Yes Sister whom God used to save His people. We know as little about her early life as we do about Rahab's. She may have been well loved and respected. But we do know her chance to make any choices about her life was stripped from her when King Xerxes took her for his harem. At a young age, she was staring at many years of being at the bidding of others.

But in that difficult situation, God gave her a voice (a very influential one at that) and a message she alone was suited to share (Esther 4:14). Her courage to approach the king, not once but twice, at the risk of death proved that her freedom was in God. She shows us that the control of others does not limit God.

God still works yeses when circumstances say we're stuck in what appears to be a permanent no. Other human beings can trample on all that is precious and unique to us, but God can give us back an even greater yes.

The yes God gave Esther saved her own life, her cousin Mordecai's life, and the lives of all the Jews. It stomped on evil and brought justice by uncovering an evil plot.

Ruth

We read about gentle Ruth in the Old Testament book with her name. (Are you noticing the precedent God set for the mighty ways He works through women?)

Ruth maintained her God-given spark and walked through loss with dignity and faith, refusing to give in to victimhood. She lost her husband and her livelihood. She had no children and was far away from her own people. Back then, those realities meant a bleak future. Even so, Ruth opted to care for her widowed mother-in-law, Naomi, committing to a lifetime as the widow's Yes Sister.

Ruth modeled for us how to lean on God and trust Him with the future. Her confidence that God would be enough directed her thoughts, attitudes, behavior, tone, motives, hope, endurance, faithfulness, steadiness, emotions, generosity, outlook, wisdom, and boldness.

Her economic descent did not define her. Her suffering did not define her. Ridicule and scorn from others did not define her. Those things *could not* define her. They did not have the permission or authority or power to do so.

She did not measure her worth based on social status. Her treasure was not of this world. Instead, her worth was in belonging to God. Her wealth was the heritage of God. And her treasure was God Himself.

As a result, uncertainty did not undo her.

Loss did not destroy her.

Drastic change for the worse did not defeat her.

And it was not because of who Ruth was but because she relied on God's constant and overriding yes in her life. She obeyed and lived as a Yes Sister.

If I could turn back time and offer Yes Sister wisdom to my younger self, these truths from Ruth's story would top my "remember this" list. Living rooted by ever-deepening faith in God guides everything.

Ruth wasn't thinking, *I'm going to be a Yes Sister to women thousands of years from now by staying with Naomi and offering myself to Boaz. And I'll bet God will send the Messiah through my descendants.*

She had no idea the extent of what God was doing with her life! But Ruth is an example of how to walk with Him every day, how to live a quiet and well-lived life committed to the Lord.

And like Ruth, we don't know the fullness of how He will work through our lives either. But one day He will reveal it all.

God's yes was all Rahab, Esther, and Ruth had going for them. But it was the best yes, which they passed on to us without realizing how immeasurable its impact would be.

Still Others

- Sarah, Rebekah, Rachel: three matriarchs of the Hebrew people
- Hannah, who received the gift of her son from God as an answer to relentless prayer
- Deborah, prophetess and judge who led her people into battle
- Elizabeth, John the Baptist's mother
- Mary, Jesus's mother

We know some of these women lived with brokenness. Remember, God does powerful things through broken people who've lived with a lot of nos.

Sarah, Rebekah, and Rachel were the wives of Abraham, Isaac, and Jacob. All three first mothers of God's people were unable to conceive children for many years.

It's difficult for us to grasp the level of shame those ancient women endured because of their culture's idea that a woman's worth and respectability came through bearing children. She had no other purpose as far as society was concerned back then.

But God told Abraham that He would grow an entire nation through his offspring. Even though Sarah and Abraham's inability to conceive appeared to be a no, it was all part of God's yes in His timing.

Hannah was another woman who prayed incessantly for God to give her a child and to release her from the torment of her husband's other wife, who had several children. Hannah didn't have an easy go of it. Finally, God gave her Samuel, whom she dedicated to His service. And then He gave her more children as well.

The women's lives were marked by years and years of nos. Their only hope was that God would fill the huge holes in their hearts. And He did. He could have changed their dreams, removed their desires. He didn't have to make Abraham that promise, but by fulfilling it, He showed that He speaks directly into our pained places.

I didn't grow up surrounded by cheerleaders who urged me to launch a magazine because I obviously had what it took to accomplish it. Quite the contrary. If the question "Who should we call to take on this project?" had been posed to my entire hometown, it's a good guess my name wouldn't have come up! And that's fine, I'm realizing, because even though I work hard, God has made everything happen. From the start, He's been responsible.

Odds against us don't matter a whit when God purposes to do something. And take heart, sister, He has beautiful purposes for you.

God's intentions for some women involve positions of great influence. Deborah the judge kept the faith as she helped the Israelite military commander Barak lead Israel to victory. Her steady faith in God during a critical time made her a successful leader.

In the New Testament, we find Elizabeth. She was the mother of John the Baptist, who paved the way for his cousin Jesus. After being unable to conceive (yes, her too), Elizabeth was finally pregnant when her younger relative Mary came to visit her.

Mary had recently learned she, too, was expecting a special child from God. Mary was probably still processing the angel's words to her that her boy would be "Son of the Most High" (Luke 1:32) and God would give Him the throne of His ancestor David. She found comfort and encouragement from sharing that time with Elizabeth.

Each of these women was an unlikely pick for how God worked through her:

The infertile and too old gave birth to children.

The disgraced became part of Jesus's lineage.

The woman leader of great faith guided the Israelites to victory.

The too young and insignificant mothered the Savior.

Together they reach out to us and show us what's possible. If someone once communed with the Lord that closely, we can have that kind of relationship with Him too. We learn from these Yes Sisters of the Bible that seeking the Lord with the treasures of our hearts is how we experience His blessing. In knowing Him, we refill and find new strength. We also learn to pay heed to our everyday lives that will impact our Yes Sisters to come.

We could discuss so many more Yes Sisters of the Bible if we had the space. The point is, God works through Yes Sisters. He is not finished with our stories.

> Therefore, since we are surrounded by so great a cloud of witnesses, let us also . . . run with endurance the race that is set before us, looking to Jesus, the founder and perfecter of our faith. (Heb. 12:1–2 ESV)

A WORD FROM
a Yes Sister

Wilisha Scaife, *family-community engagement liaison and instructor at Ball State University*

At His Feet and in His Face: The Principle of Priority

One of my favorite "sista stories" is the story of Mary and Martha (Luke 10:38–42).

Some people misunderstand this story, as if Jesus was rebuking Martha. No. Mary and Martha give us *the principle of priority*.

As women, we are to demonstrate *both*: worship (sitting at His feet) and work (service). I believe the call is to be both Martha and Mary. It is a matter of priority.

As women, we are prone to work first—in our homes, in our communities, and in the church. It is easy for us to neglect time at His feet and in His face! Yes, we should work, but our work should be our *worship overflow*.

When our work comes before (or in place of) our worship, not only is our work in vain, but it is usually not done in the right spirit. Ever met a "church worker" with an ugly attitude? The whole time they are working and serving, they frown, gripe, and complain. This is not the offering God desires.

But when we seek to be more like Him (do things His way) and have His attitude and character (Matt. 6:33), we serve out of our surrender and sanctification. Yes, faith without works is dead (James 2:17), but the only *faith work* that counts is "faith which worketh by love" (Gal. 5:6 KJV).

My service to God and His people should be motivated and energized by love (His overwhelming love for me and my loving response to it).

Chapter 21

A Celebration of Yes Sisters

This day shall be for you a memorial day, and you shall keep it as a feast to the LORD; throughout your generations, as a statute forever, you shall keep it as a feast.

Exodus 12:14 ESV

I stood in the banquet room, surrounded by women who'd come to celebrate hope and the connections that bonded us. I wanted to see concretely that what my sisters have helped make possible really is touching lives.

That night in 2015 marked a milestone. The conference celebrated our vision at *HOPE for Women* magazine. It remains a memorial for me to look back on with gratitude for the Lord and all my Yes Sisters who brought me back from my life of no.

Publishing online and print magazines gives me opportunities daily to encourage and be encouraged by the sisters I know in person and those I haven't met but my heart has related to through their words. But keeping a magazine going doesn't give me opportunities to spend personal time with most of the women in this *HOPE* tribe. That can make me feel distant from them.

That conference night in Muncie, Indiana, changed all that.

The whole room was elegant—the tables, the chairs, the walls. Everyone was dressed beautifully. My mother and daughter and so many friends and supporters mingled with one another, many meeting for the first time. Only God knows how many bonds were formed or deepened that night.

Several women spoke, including me. I don't remember all that I said, but I still get goose bumps remembering how I felt. My old life was fading into another, better one that was strengthening its roots every week. I knew I even looked different. The vibrancy I felt inside couldn't keep from glowing on my face and showing in the way I carried myself.

●●●

The verse from Exodus at the beginning of this chapter records the Lord addressing Moses when He explained the meaning of the Passover. It was directed to Moses specifically for the people of Israel, whom God was going to draw out of Egypt and lead to freedom in a land of their own. Its theme applies to us as well, because each day marks a memorial of yes in the Lord's plans for us.

Moses's story was epic. It was filled with more than a few magnanimous yeses and resounding nos.

The Hebrew men and women had endured slavery in Egypt for longer than they had the energy to keep counting. Hour after hour, day after day, decade after decade, they toiled under the Egyptians' brutal treatment.

Moses was the Hebrew baby God pulled from their midst to be raised by Pharaoh's daughter. God had saved him with a big yes and said no to Pharaoh's efforts to kill Moses along with the other Hebrew baby boys. And God allowed Moses to secretly maintain a relationship with his biological family at least for a few years while his mother nursed him. But those saving nos and yeses came with the price of his not really belonging with either nation.

Instead of suffering with the Israelites, Moses grew up in privilege. While his birth family struggled under Pharaoh's leadership, Moses lived in luxury. He never hungered or yelled in agony at the flick of a whip on his back. He gained position, education, and power. But all of that did not make him Egyptian. It did, however, make him very different from the Israelites.

When he was grown, his conflicting identities became problematic and led to his impulsive decision to defend an Israelite whom an Egyptian was beating. Killing the Egyptian was an act that ushered in years of alienation from both heritages. It could be considered a long season of no for him. But God was still writing history and had His best yeses in store.

Eventually, God spoke to Moses through a burning bush, of all things, and sent him back to Egypt to lead the people out of slavery. Moses's past mix of yeses and nos had fit him for the leadership role God had in store for him. His higher education in Pharaoh's palace provided him with knowledge of the culture and geography, as well as organizational and management skills. And his familiarity in the palace helped him gain access to the new pharaoh's ear.

Moses's first request to let the Israelites go was met with an unequivocal no from Pharaoh. In fact, the more Moses obeyed God, the worse things got for God's people. Pharaoh's nos grew more powerful and defiant, despite plague after horrible plague that God sent on the Egyptians and their animals, land, water, and homes.

And then the Lord instructed Moses about the tenth plague that was about to strike. This plague would receive the biggest no of all from Pharaoh. But Almighty God would silence Pharaoh with His most powerful *NO!* in return.

God told Moses to instruct the people to smear the blood of young lambs on the doorframes of their homes. Any home marked like this would escape the tenth plague that would kill every firstborn male in the land. The Israelites obeyed, and their sons were spared. But every firstborn Egyptian son died during the night. Imagine the wailing of the Egyptian mothers and fathers!

The Passover celebration referred to in Exodus 12:14 commemorates the saving yes that God worked for His people, because the angel of death passed over their homes.

Why am I referring to this particular story—Moses's story—in a book for women? Because God has the last word regarding those who belong to Him, and that word is *yes*.

When God changed His people's legacy of no, He instructed them to memorialize it with celebrations future generations could never forget. Celebrations that would boost their faith over and over despite imminent hardships.

The end of a past full of nos and the beginning of a future full of yeses are reasons to celebrate—deliberately, in community, and regularly. We Yes Sisters are in this together, and we need one another to remind us that our stories are not finished.

One day all who are His will hear yes and only yes forever and always, without end. In the meantime, the examples of Rahab, Esther, Ruth, and all the others model for us how to live the Lord's yes despite the nos on this earth.

Our sisters before us set the pace. It's our turn to join them. Today is tomorrow's history, and our younger sisters are learning from us.

I've faced struggles, losses, and challenges since that celebration night at the conference. The meek-hearted little girl I once was is still part of me, but as I heal, I care for her more effectively. I can look back at the bumpy path of my life with hope, as the good and the bad have been worthwhile because of the growth they have caused. God has redeemed so many nos for me. The future will bring more, I have no doubt. But every yes He has granted through each Yes Sister reinforces my belief in His love for me. In that, I am secure.

These days I still look in the mirror and see wholeness radiating in my smile, which comes easily now. Seeing myself this way keeps me celebrating every day, and I live to invite other women to keep celebrating true life and lasting yes.

Join with me in responding with a big ol' heart-lifting, legacy-changing *yes!*

A WORD FROM
a Yes Sister

Candace Cameron Bure, *actress and author*

The Faithful Yes

I work in an industry in which I'm often surrounded by many negative influences. But I look at it as an incredible opportunity to be a light in a dark world.

If we dwell on the negatives and the hardships of life, I don't think we would ever want to wake up each morning and get out of bed. When we've got God on our side, seeing those negative influences as a mission field gives a whole new perspective on living.

I absolutely believe Christian integrity can be maintained in Hollywood—or in anyone's challenging workplace or neighborhood or friendship. I remain focused by keeping my priorities in line when it comes to my faith . . . church, small group Bible study each week, and time daily with the Lord in prayer.

Most of all, with every decision I make—every conversation, every response to a friend, every word I speak to a Yes Sister—I ask myself, "Would this be pleasing to God?" If I can't think of a single way it could benefit the kingdom or give glory to God, I will most likely say no, stay silent, or look for a way to say what needs to be said with love as my motivation rather than my own interests. And I have my husband, my family, and my trusted, close friends to keep me accountable.

I definitely attribute the strength in relationships to the Lord. When we live by the principles God laid out as a blueprint for us, it absolutely works. When conflicts arise, whether in a friendship or my marriage, we always go to the Bible and resolve it. We try to honor each other and put each other's needs before our own. We're saying His Yes to each other. But what that really means is that we're saying yes to Him.

Notes

Chapter 9 We CAN Create Our Dreams

1. Bruce Wilkinson, *The Dream Giver* (Sister, OR: Multnomah, 2003), 13–14.
2. Wilkinson, *Dream Giver*, 15.
3. Wilkinson, *Dream Giver*, 14–15.
4. Wilkinson, *Dream Giver*, 17.
5. Priscilla Shirer, *Awaken: 90 Days with the God Who Speaks* (Nashville: B&H, 2017), Day 64.

Chapter 10 We WILL Overcome

1. Dallas Willard, "The Gospel of the Kingdom and Spiritual Formation," in *The Kingdom Life: A Practical Theology of Discipleship and Spiritual Formation*, ed. Alan Andrews (Colorado Springs: NavPress, 2010), 51.

A Word from a Yes Sister A Greater Love for *The Color Purple*

1. Alice Walker, *The Color Purple* (New York: Mariner Books, 2003), 73.

Chapter 11 We DO Get Second Chances—and Thirds . . .

1. L. M. Montgomery, *Anne of Green Gables* (New York: Grosset and Dunlap, 1908), 223.
2. Montgomery, *Anne*, 34.

Chapter 13 We HAVE Shoulders to Cry On or to Stand On

1. Marilyn Vancil, *Self to Lose—Self to Find: A Biblical Approach to the Nine Enneagram Types* (Redemption Press, 2016), 7.
2. "Sir Isaac Newton," BBC, accessed July 11, 2019, http://www.bbc.co.uk/world service/learningenglish/movingwords/shortlist/newton.shtml.

Angelia L. White is the creator of *HOPE for Women* magazine, a quarterly publication with 200,000 subscribers. A Ball State University Black Alumni Award of Achievement recipient, Angelia is a mother of three and the publisher, president, and CEO of HOPE for Women, headquartered in Muncie, Indiana. Having risen from a background of discouragement, she spends her life encouraging other women to step into their full potential and share their inspiring stories.

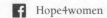

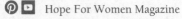